Thrive with a Hybrid Workplace

Thrive with a Hybrid Workplace

Step-by-Step Guidance from the Experts

Felice B. Ekelman, JD
and
Julie P. Kantor, PhD

ROWMAN & LITTLEFIELD
Lanham • Boulder • New York • London

Published by Rowman & Littlefield
An imprint of The Rowman & Littlefield Publishing Group, Inc.
4501 Forbes Boulevard, Suite 200, Lanham, Maryland 20706
www.rowman.com

86-90 Paul Street, London EC2A 4NE

British Library Cataloguing in Publication Information Available

Library of Congress Cataloging-in-Publication Data Available

ISBN 9781538171677 (cloth)
ISBN 9781538171684 (epub)

For our loving families and friends who cheered us on.

Contents

Acknowledgments

To begin with, we value our different perspectives and professional expertises. As a business psychologist, Julie handled the sections on leadership, productivity and wellness. As an employment attorney, Felice drove the sections on policy and guardrails. We appreciate our respective knowledge that came together to help leaders and organizations achieve best in class status.

We are most thankful for our collaborative relationship. From the moment we first started thinking about this project, we set ego aside and supported one another. We have learned so much from one another and have forged a great friendship. Inquisitiveness, good humor, and grace prevailed throughout the project.

We thank our agent and guide Maryann Karinch, who has been a critical part of our success. Maryann's patience, warmth, and knowledge made this project possible. Maryann provided expert editing and advice, and we are so grateful for the oversight she provided.

Thanks to the Rowman & Littlefield team, in particular Suzanne Staszak-Silva, for believing in us.

Over the years, we have been fortunate to have had many professional and intellectual partners who motivated us. We value their expertise and guidance and offer a shout out to our friends for lending an ear, being the counterbalance of our work, and just being there.

We also appreciate our families who have always nurtured us and encouraged us from inception to completion of this book. Thank you for knowing when to support us and when to give us space to write and connect with each other. We cherish each of you and the joy you bring to us.

We share gratitude for our clients. Our clients have taught us endless lessons, provided fantastic professional opportunities, and become our friends. Our clients brought us into their worlds, trusted us, and embraced growth and change. We have spent decades listening to clients and working with them to find answers and a way forward, and it is our clients who inspired us to take on this project. Much about the world of work has changed since we embarked on our careers, yet for all the change, many of the same problems plague leaders. For this reason, we wanted to write this book. Trust, fairness, and compassion have always been the key to successful leadership, and the quick segue we've seen to hybrid work on a broad scale has demonstrated how important these attributes are. There's still work to be done for leaders and employees as they figure out different ways to integrate their work and personal worlds both as individuals and organizations. We truly hope our efforts will advance that goal.

Introduction

The Power of And

We have served in the same professional space for years: Julie, a business psychologist advising organizations and leaders on workplace growth and development; and Felice, a workplace lawyer advising organizations and leaders on legal guidelines and risks. We have therefore often referred clients to each other: Felice to Julie when an organization she is advising has executives in need of leadership development, such as senior leaders who have been promoted and need coaching; and Julie to Felice when a leader or organization is confronting a legal complaint such as Diversity, Equity, and Inclusion (DEI) grievances based on discrimination or harassment.

Julie helps clients grow.

Felice helps clients avoid risk.

We were brought together by a mutual HR professional for a project regarding companies facing significant changes during and after the seismic shift of the COVID pandemic. She knew leaders who had no idea how to build an engaged hybrid workplace that was different from the past workplace of all hands in the office. She was concerned these changes were leading to legal and operational problems, and she knew our different perspectives together addressed questions concerning the hybrid work model. Why?

- Working from home increased.
- Leadership demands changed.
- New legal questions arose.

- Employees resisted returning to the office.
- Leaders deliberated on new work structures.
- Flexibility became the norm.
- Work as we knew it was questioned.
- Managers struggled with communication.
- Teams strove to collaborate via virtual meetings.
- Departments were challenged to re-organize with changing roles.

We shared the challenges our respective clients were coming to us with and realized they needed advice and support on the same issues *but with different perspectives*. As we saw the same clients but with different questions, we wanted to provide one-stop shopping for executives who lead hybrid organizations:

1. Policy and legal guidelines including standard legal issues you must address.
2. Leadership guidelines including diverse leadership issues and recommendations.

Leaders can make a difference in a hybrid world. As organizations toy with being more flexible, leaders need new tools to participate in the decision making and making their decisions come alive. We wanted to provide those tools.

And so, this book was born.

We begin by agreeing with business consultant Deborah Schroeder-Saulnier, who spotlights the power of *and* over *or* in her book *The Power of Paradox*. In short, the best solution is often the one that combines seemingly competing ideas rather than picking one over the other.

Welcome to the hybrid workplace!

One ongoing debate of the business world is this: remote or office? Our goal is to help leaders resolve this debate by saying *and* so that you and your teams embrace hybrid. Our follow-on goal is then to make it work.

The great debate of remote versus office begins with the myth of the separate worlds we all live in: work life and personal life. For centuries, work and home were separated by physically going to and from an office. The separation was actually a myth, because we went between two different locations, but each of us was still one person. Our bosses may have not known anything about our family or friends and vice versa, but we did. Two worlds. One person.

The wall between our worlds has been slowly coming down due to diverse factors: first and foremost, technological advances. There are also factors such as globalization, generational differences, dual-career couples, commitments to causes, or people just wanting "to bring their whole self to work." The COVID pandemic beginning in 2020 pretty much sealed the deal. The days of all employees reporting to work every day are gone. Hybrid work is here to stay.

Our goal is to provide organizations, leaders, and employees with guidance as to how to sort through what feels like a ping-pong argument about whether to embrace a hybrid workplace by dispensing with reporting to an office every day or to stick with the more conventional approach of reporting to an office five days a week. Some leaders claim corporate culture cannot survive without an office where people spend time together in person on a regular basis. Other leaders claim togetherness is not all that important and does not result in greater productivity or creativity. We've read the views of commentators who proclaim the debate over working remotely is a culture war: old-guard baby boomers versus newer generations of employees.

As the air clears in this great debate, organizations can take a series of action steps.

1. Decide whether to create a flexible workplace.
2. Define workplace flexibility.
3. Ensure the decision is successful.

Step 3 means identifying the skills that are necessary for leaders to succeed in managing a workplace where some or all employees work away from an office on a regular basis. Leaders can learn to navigate the different challenges that come with working virtually some or all of the time as well as how to develop a cohesive team, generate and sustain camaraderie, and accomplish business goals.

Where and when should white-collar workers work? Our advice is to be flexible and thoughtful!

The debate regarding flexible work arrangements will continue to rage. As reliable broadband becomes ubiquitous and technological advances create even better tools to collaborate virtually, the options available to organizations to implement flexible work policies will continue to evolve. But the skills needed to survive in a work world where remote work is increasingly the workplace of choice need to be identified and honed. Our goal is to provide leaders with a pathway. We intend to help you

- understand flexible work options, and how to assess which options are best for your organization
- develop a thoughtful approach to hybrid work that is consistent with your organization's core values
- identify how to best lead in hybrid work environments with the tools and competence to succeed
- identify pitfalls that may hinder success in implementing hybrid work protocols from both an individual and an enterprise point of view

What is your starting point? *Intentionality.* That is, leaving little to chance. Perhaps the opposite of winging it. Providing direction and then repeating that direction. Communicating in an organized fashion—meaning planning, training, and repeating the process. And then revisiting and improving on that process.

In 2021 we spoke with the leader of a sixty-five-person team in the financial services industry. Before March 2020, her team was office first with a few remote employees spread around the globe. In 2020 as her team and the entire organization worked remotely, the organization announced several return-to-work plans, each of which was based on a split-shift approach. The plans (or rumors of the plans) were announced then postponed as the pandemic seesawed in its severity.

Despite the postponements, the organization was losing the retention battle. Employees had moved away from their office or just plain liked remote work. Her organization had failed to garner employee support (much less enthusiasm) in its attempts to woo staff back to work with flexible split-shift arrangements. Employees were moving to other financial services firms that promised remote-first environments with no obligation to live near an office. Faced with the reality that employees were not embracing a split-shift arrangement, the organization backed off.

That's not the end of this story. During the 2020 shutdown, this organization had made great strides in making remote work meaningful.

So, while most of the workforce was working remotely, the company achieved success developing protocols for a remote workplace. The key to this success? Intentionality. Leaders in this organization were taught to overcommunicate, to be empathetic, to look closely at schedules, and to better coordinate the team's activities so that the focus was on accomplishing immediate tasks.

There's a lot we can learn from this organization, and it all starts with intentionality. The 7 Cs of leadership, which are the focus of section II of this book, embody the conception of intentionality.

For many of us who experienced working from home exclusively for the first time during the 2020 lockdowns, the transition to work from home exposed both the tension between work life and life life and the ease with which many white-collar jobs could be performed remotely. Out of necessity, remote work became the norm. As we move from the necessity of working remotely and into the paradigm of choice, we have the opportunity to choose among the myriad flexible arrangements that exist.

The staying power of hybrid work cannot be disputed. Consider one snapshot: From October 19 to October 29, 2021 (a calmish moment during the COVID 19 pandemic rollercoaster), a survey of Manhattan office workers revealed that only 8 percent of office workers were reporting to work every day of the workweek while 54 percent were still fully remote. Of the remaining 38 percent, 10 percent were in the office four days a week, 12 percent were in the office three days per week, 8 percent were in the office two days a week, and 8 percent were in the office one day per week.[1]

A broader survey, which covered a larger cross section of workers in the United States from May 2020 through the first calendar quarter of 2021, documents the shift to working from home and predicts that American workers will supply about 20 percent of full workdays from home in the post-pandemic economy.[2] That is one day at home on average assuming a five-day workweek. This research report cites data indicating that the boom in work-from-home arrangements resulted in a 5 percent productivity boost in the post-pandemic economy due to re-optimized work arrangements. Whether that boost is permanent is yet to be seen, but these studies combined with anecdotal reports point to one conclusion: Employers who insist on an office-only protocol for white-collar workers will be in the minority. Hybrid work arrangements are here to stay. Leaders should be informed and intentional as they choose an approach to flexible work, anticipate issues, train managers, and revisit their decisions.

Our point of view: Embrace flexible options! As you have already discerned, our recommendation is for enterprises to consider hybrid work with an open mind, implement well-thought-out policies and protocols, and remain positioned to attract the best and brightest—wherever they may live. Organizations need to acknowledge that hybrid work is the new norm and recognize that the challenge is for leaders to ensure that remote work is inclusive, meaningful, and productive. Organizations need to accept the notion that if they fail to adapt a flexible approach to remote work and empower leaders to make decisions regarding how work is performed, they will lose the race for the best talent. We are in a work world where white-collar employees expect to be provided with options. The ability to work remotely at least some of the time is now a given.

For organizations reluctant to let their people go and work from home, a new level and style of trust is mandatory. Trust is critical as is dispensing with the adage that presence in the office equals productivity. Ideally, leaders trust employees to do their job without constant visual oversight. Measuring commitment and success now requires leaders to better identify responsibilities and goals so that individual contributors who may not be reporting to an office in person every day can be fairly evaluated and recognized.

Organizations should carefully choose an appropriate—and flexible—work policy, one that enables leaders to lead and manage without limiting the organization's ability to attract qualified candidates, retain valued contributors, and create a culture in which employees can thrive. As our readers will learn in the pages that follow, we urge leaders to evaluate their approach to where and when work is performed alongside their core values. Developing and then articulating an approach to work will be easier to accomplish when viewed alongside your organization's larger goals. We also urge leaders to recognize that approaches will change over time. Recalibration is an important part of the process and is not an admission that a mistake was made. Our workplace world is evolving at an ever-quickening speed, and in years to come our organizations will need to adjust policies to reflect changes in the world of work.

We urge leaders to embrace what is now referred to as the hybrid workplace. Organizations that aspire to be best-in-class employers need to intentionally develop strategies to make hybrid arrangements workable and meaningful. That means providing the flexibility employees want and attracting engaged and knowledgeable leaders who are armed with the skills needed to manage hybrid teams. These skills will not always come naturally to managers. Leaders are encouraged to provide tools and support to learn how to develop trust with employees so that employees can be confident that their work is being assessed fairly and they are provided with the mentoring opportunities that once were provided exclusively in person. You will see the word *intentionality* throughout the chapters that follow. Intentionality must govern the decisions that frame hybrid work policies. Intentionality can govern how leaders manage their teams, meaning that leaders should be trained to recognize when work can be asynchronous (performed independently without immediate responses from others) and when work must be collaborative. Business enterprises should be alert to the various pitfalls that can arise if the transformation to hybrid is not well planned and understand the importance of approaching the new workplace in a thoughtful manner. In the chapters that follow, we explore ways to lead a hybrid team and will provide guidance that addresses the real-world challenges that both leaders and team members who are not always in the same place at the same time experience. We also emphasize the need for recalibration as enterprises, leaders, and employees all recognize that nothing is permanent. We are experiencing a transformation in how we work, where we work, and when we work. Learning to thrive with change is never easy, but workplace change is happening at an accelerating pace. Many of us need to step back, recognize our biases, and learn to accept change with an open mind (and heart). An approach that is effective today may need to be tweaked tomorrow.

Our evolving workplace will also include employees who are evolving. We now know that there is no separation between work and life, and employees will continue to want to bring their "whole self to work" regardless of where and when they work. Where the work is done is a big issue; when the work is done is also an issue. As employees strive to maximize effectiveness at work, they also need to maintain boundaries and balance between work and life. As a leader, you will need to meet the needs of employees and organizational needs simultaneously.

We present options and a way forward to understand the changing world of work, to dispense with old biases, and to establish trust between the enterprise, its leaders, and its employees. This is an exciting moment in the world of work, but transformation is never easy.

And so, we begin!

Section I

PLANNING AND PREPARING A HYBRID WORK POLICY

A hybrid work approach combines on-premises and remote models and creates an environment where team members alternate time in the office with remote work. *Hybrid* means flexible, with a slew of permutations on the hybrid model. No matter what protocol an enterprise adopts, clear policies—in writing—are a must. No policy need be etched in stone and forever. To the contrary: Organizations should let employees know that policies are subject to change—and there is a legal reason for that if employees are covered by a collective bargaining agreement.

First and foremost, when dissecting the concept of hybrid work, it is easy to conflate two concepts: *where* work is performed and *when* work is performed. The conversation about remote work tends to mix the two together. Where work is performed is typically the central focus of the hybrid work discussion.

When work is performed is a reasonable outgrowth of the location debate. If I can work from home, why do I have to work only from 9 a.m. to 5 p.m. (or whatever my typical work hours are)? The *when* question is increasingly a critical part of the analysis. As enterprises decide how much freedom to provide employees about where they work, the freedom to work anywhere leads to the question "If I can work wherever I like, why can't I work whenever I like?"

Who decides where and when should never come down to one person's preferences, analysis of options, or worldview—unless that one person wants to invite trouble. Depending on the size of the organization, the answer might be "a team involving everyone" or "a team reflecting the composition of the company."

Once the possible answers to where, when, and who are explored, a leader is then able to launch the effort of crafting a hybrid work policy.

Chapter One

Where and When Work Is Performed and Who Decides

A hybrid workplace is one where employees are expected to work away from the office on a regular basis. This simple definition allows us to discuss a range of different approaches to hybrid work while staying true to the definition.

WHERE WORK IS PERFORMED

A hybrid environment can take many forms, but it essentially means that some employees work remotely at least some of the time. The arrangement could look like any of these options.

- Remote work is the primary protocol with occasional meetings in person.
- Employees work from the office on certain days and from home the remainder of the week.
- Employees work from the office for part of the month then at home for the rest of the month.
- Employees alternate office and remote workdays.
- Every employee chooses when to work from home and when to work from the office.
- Some employees work remotely all the time while others work in an office regularly or on a hybrid basis.

THE OFFICE-FIRST WORKPLACE

An office-first workplace is what you think of when recalling a traditional workplace where every employee commutes to a physical location each day and has an assigned workstation. In the office-first environment, the expectation is that work is performed in the office (except of course if visiting a customer or other stakeholder). Typically, the expectation is every employee will take a seat at their workstation every day. In an office-first environment, employees find it comforting to know that the same chair awaits them in the same spot next to the same colleagues each day. We are creatures of habit, and the daily routine of hanging up a coat, stowing a bag, and getting the morning coffee are all small pleasures that come with the routine of office-based work.

The term *office first* has been adopted as a short-hand way to explain an enterprise's approach to where work is performed. Whether there are opportunities for employees to work away from the office is a matter of policy, but *office first* means employees should understand that they will need to commute to the office all the time or some of the time. The office-first approach messages to employees and applicants that they will need to live within commuting distance of their office. The term also connotes an expectation that leaders will be leading from the office all or some of the time.

The office-first environment does not preclude remote work. Even in an office-first environment, your organization may allow remote work. As white-collar employees increasingly expect greater flexibility in where they may work, enterprises that adhere to the office-first paradigm will be forced to reckon with demands for exceptions to the rule.

Remote-work policies in an office-first environment can run the gamut but typically fall into two categories: (1) exceptions for some employees who work exclusively remotely; and (2) exceptions when hybrid work arrangements are permitted.

REMOTE-ONLY EMPLOYEES IN AN OFFICE-FIRST WORKPLACE: THE DISTRIBUTED WORKFORCE

The first typical exception to the office-first paradigm is when your enterprise identifies particular positions as remote eligible. Generally, there are two reasons an enterprise might make an exception to requiring in-office work. First, the nature of the work performed by certain employees lends itself to remote work: think salespersons whose duties require frequent travel or who must cover a geographic area where an office is not located. For example, your enterprise operates out of one office but has a nationwide network of customer accounts. Sales staff might live and work throughout the country and never report to an office.

The second category of remote worker who might be an exception to an office-first workplace are those employees who have a skill for which a wider recruiting net must be cast. Particularly in moments when the labor market is tight, your enterprise might have little choice but to identify positions as remote eligible because it is unable to recruit and retain talent in the location where it maintains an office. Contributors like programmers, for example, may be difficult to recruit and have little reason to work alongside other colleagues in the same location.

Long before the advent of Wi-Fi and laptops, remote work existed, often on an ad hoc basis. For decades, managers working at global companies have long managed teams that include remote workers who may be based in different countries. There are countless circumstances where organizations that are office-first have long employed individuals who never report to an office. What's changed is that now the rest of the workforce is tuned in to the possibility of remote work on a long-term basis, as are employees who were not previously eligible for remote work but experienced (and liked the experience of) remote work during the 2020 shutdowns. These employees, if mandated to work exclusively in an office, will question why some positions are designated remote eligible and others are not. This is an important concept discussed extensively in upcoming chapters on crafting a hybrid work policy.

OCCASIONAL PART-TIME REMOTE EMPLOYEES IN AN OFFICE-FIRST ENVIRONMENT (LIMITED HYBRID WORK SCHEDULES)

The second typical hybrid option to the office-first environment is a policy permitting some or all employees to work remotely. An example is a policy that permits work from home once a week or for a few days a month. This approach is different from the split-shift approach that we discuss later because here remote work is permitted only on an occasional (as opposed to a regular) basis. We have observed enterprises increasingly adopting policies that permit employees to work from home sometimes as a reaction to pressure to provide the greater flexibility that white-collar workers are increasingly demanding. Policies permitting occasional work from home should be carefully crafted to ensure that employees understand what is permitted and leaders can enforce the policies consistently. Policies vary and can require advance notice or authorization to work from home for a day or may limit the number of days that can be worked from home.

Historically many organizations have tried to limit the scope of work-from-home policies because of fear that they will lose control of their staff; their communications will be hindered; they will not be able to monitor productivity; or their leaders will not be able to maintain a connection with employees who are not physically in the workplace. Logistical issues also arise—for example, if an employee is permitted to work from home on occasion, does this justify the cost associated with providing a laptop and other necessary technology to support both remote and office-based work? We urge leaders to re-examine their hesitancy. After all, most white-collar workers spent months working from home exclusively in 2020 and often with surprising effectiveness. As noted in the introduction, managing a hybrid workplace successfully requires *intentionality*. Learn how to oversee a distributed workforce if this is new to you. Likewise, commit to understanding how to get the most out of a hybrid schedule. Make sure that when your employees are not engaged in virtual meetings, they are engaged in interpersonal collaborative activities.

THE REAL HYBRID: THE SPLIT-SHIFT APPROACH

You may have heard the term *split shift*. This typically refers to a protocol where time is split fairly evenly between home and office. The split can take the form of several days each week away from the office or one or more weeks each month away from the office. With a split schedule, employees are expected to report to an office regularly but not every day—hence, flexibility characterizes the split-shift approach. Schedules can be fixed, or they can change each week.

Employees might report to the office only when they have a reason to be in the office, with some minimum in-person attendance required or expected. For example, your organization might offer a hybrid schedule in which employees are expected to report to an office for regular, in-person meetings but have no obligation to work in an office on any other occasion. The permutations are endless.

The critical component of a split-shift arrangement is that employees are not expected in the office every day, but they are expected to live within commuting distance so that they are able to report to the office on a regular basis. A split shift reduces commuting time and expense and provides employees with the opportunity to be home more of the time. Yet a split shift still provides the benefits of working side-by-side with coworkers on a regular basis. Leaders may or may not have the same flexibility (again this can vary by organization) to work both at home and in the office. But with a split-shift arrangement, leaders are challenged by navigating their teams' schedules and learning to oversee a team that's both in and out.

Room for All versus Hoteling

Hoteling is a natural outgrowth of the split-shift approach that has become increasingly popular. In recent years employers have experimented with and, in some cases, embraced the concept.

Hoteling is a form of office space management. It eliminates traditional, assigned workspace for some or all staff. Employees report for work to an office but do not have their own assigned workstation and, instead, may work at a variety of spaces. Booking technology is often used by companies who use the hoteling concept so that the employee books a workstation on a day-to-day basis. With booking technology, each booked day employees bring their work materials with them (or retrieve them from a locker) and carry them to their reserved workstation.

Hoteling can enhance space utilization and enable businesses to reduce their office footprint, saving rent costs. Enormous savings can be reaped from a smaller real estate obligation. Right sizing the workplace can also reduce your organization's carbon footprint, creating a positive environmental impact. The market is filled with booking technology options that enable employees to choose from calibrated workstations and even conference rooms that include the necessary technology to perform whatever tasks might be anticipated.

Advocates claim hoteling enhances collaboration because employees don't sit next to the same colleagues every day. Instead, they work alongside different coworkers, thereby enhancing the opportunity to network and collaborate. Hoteling can result in new contacts within an organization. Does this provide an organic way to strengthen community? Does hoteling enhance socialization because employees meet different colleagues on a regular basis? We've yet to see a body of scientific study confirming these claims, but it does seem likely that employees who are exposed to a wider group of colleagues will have an enhanced socialization experience.

With a hoteling arrangement there is room for every employee scheduled to work in an office at the same time. That workstation might change or might be shared, but regardless of the physical arrangement, there is room for everyone in the office when your employees report for work.

Some organizations find that hoteling increases engagement because employees are regularly mixing it up. Forcing employees to sit with others they may not know may create those water-cooler moments when employees who might not interact in the workplace meet and presumably discuss their roles. Critics of the hoteling concept claim these daily changes are disruptive because there is no predictability in the work experience. Hoteling usually means open-floor workplaces, which do not provide privacy, and employees may find the constant change unnerving. And given that employees need to be assigned lockers for their personal belongings, this requires additional space and additional time to manage each day. Whether hoteling contributes to collaboration is not easy to tell, but it is popular in many workplaces where not everyone must report to the office every day, because fewer workstations are required.

THE REMOTE-FIRST WORKPLACE

Moving toward the other end of the spectrum we find the remote-first approach. Here too there are many permutations.

First there's the no-office workplace. This is the completely remote option. Employees can work anywhere, and your organization can hire employees who live anywhere.

Now we add an optional office. With this option, there is an office—or perhaps many. While an office or two or three may exist, employees are not expected to report to a physical office ever. Employees need not live in the vicinity of an office.

Then there's yet another approach. Your organization may maintain offices everywhere employees are located, even though reporting to the office is optional. In this model, your organization may focus its hiring on certain geographic hubs so that employees have the option to work with others. With this model, the remote-first organization's employees are not expected to report to the office except when requested to do so—for example, when in-person collaboration is deemed necessary for a project or meeting. With a remote-centric approach, the office design typically focuses on creating shared spaces for collaboration. Companies that embrace a remote-first approach and maintain offices will often create spaces that are open with a focus on areas for meetings and the necessary technology for conducting meetings that include individuals both on-site and remote. Some companies may include individual workstations for some of their staff—for example, employees who may want to work in the office or employees who live outside commuting distance from the office and are visiting. A remote-first approach can also accommodate employees who live near the office and want to work there on a regular basis rather than at home.

Yet another and increasingly popular approach to the remote-first workplace is for an enterprise to maintain physical offices in locations where clusters of employees live. This approach still meets the definition of a remote-first environment because employees are not expected to report to an office to work, but it provides a meeting place for those employees who want to get out of the house, meet colleagues, or conduct a meeting in person.

Then there are *coworking spaces*, that is, spaces developed by a third party that cater to organizations seeking flexibility. Coworking spaces allow organizations to provide a space for employees to meet that may be closer to where employees live than an office in the commercial district of a city center: think a suburban space in addition to or in lieu of a downtown location that provides employees with a place to meet that may be more convenient (and less costly to lease) than a space in a city center.

Why would a remote-first organization spend resources on an office? Employees like having choices. The ability to work from home on days when they are in virtual meetings all day or performing tasks that require a high degree of concentration might be appreciated, yet at the same time the ability to see colleagues and collaborate in person sometimes is important to people, so the concept of a remote-first workplace with the ability to work in person with others can be very appealing. We think that this approach to the remote-first workplace will become popular.

WHEN WORK IS PERFORMED

Reimagining work is not simply challenging the norms of the physical workplace. Increasingly organizations are considering new approaches to when work is performed. This is not a new concept. Consider the press that Patagonia received in 2016 when *Let My People Go Surfing* was published by author Yvon Chouinard. *Let My People Go Surfing* recounts the history of Patagonia, a US–based outdoor clothing and equipment company. The book details Patagonia's long-term commitment to allowing and encouraging its employees to work flexible hours as long as they do their work, which is the point of the title: If the surf's good, surf now and work later. In 2016 this was an outlier approach. Not so much now. Let's admit it. For some white-collar workers, this flexibility always existed even when we were chained to an office and never considered working from home (except on a snow day or when ill). But for most white-collar workers, someone was checking to see that they logged in at nine and did not leave before five.

Like a hybrid work policy, a flexible work schedule is increasingly viewed by employees as an employee benefit. It is not unusual particularly for start-ups to boast that they provide employees with the freedom to work when they like. Websites include language like "Savor workplace flexibility: Morning person? Night owl? We don't enforce a rigid 9-to-5, so you can get your work done on a schedule that's best for you and your family."[1] A flexible approach to when work is done is one way to respond to employees whose personal circumstances are such that they prefer to work during hours that match their children's school day or for employees who just work better early or later in the day when they focus best. For those employers who are considering a flexible hour program, such a program can be implemented in an office-first, hybrid, or remote-first environment. *When* employees work is not constrained by *where* employees work. (Except of course that most employers and employees are not comfortable knowing that an employee is working alone overnight in an office building.)

As the hybrid workplace became increasingly popular as a demanded term and condition of employment, commentators began opining on whether *work from home* meant work from home whenever you like. *Hybrid work* has become a catch-all term for flexible approaches to white-collar work, but managing remote work and managing work schedules are two very different things. It is important to address questions of flexibility as to *when* work is performed as a separate issue from *where* the work is performed.

Does it matter when work is performed? That should be an easy question for a leader to answer, but it is not. Most white-collar jobs require that employees be present during business hours to communicate with colleagues, customers, vendors, and other third parties with whom they must engage. But other work—drafting written materials, analyzing data and information, reviewing emails and documents—can be performed outside traditional business hours—except perhaps when the work is time sensitive.

Business leaders can approach flexible work schedules in an enlightened way. Why should employees whose duties do not require that they be tethered to a 9–5 schedule work set hours? Every enterprise should communicate a reasonable approach to its employees that enables employees to manage their workload as well as their life. This should be an approach that applies to on-site and remote workers alike.

Naysayers will always have a reason to reject change. Leaders might worry that just when you need someone, they are not responding; or that managing the schedules of so many team members will be a full-time job; or that collaboration and productivity will suffer when everyone is not working at the same time.

There are cons to complete flexibility of course. One danger in permitting employees to self-schedule their work and decide when they wish to work as opposed to reporting to work during designated hours is the heightened risk of proximity bias. If the employee is not at their virtual (or on-site) desk during traditional business hours, their leader might wonder if that employee is working. As we will discuss later when covering diversity, equity, and inclusion (DEI), proximity bias is the incorrect assumption that people will produce better work if they are physically present in their office and if managers can see they are performing their job. A related misconception is that the employee who is working remotely or working on their own schedule is not really working. We strongly urge leaders to recognize that the introduction of remote work in an organization must be accompanied by an intentional effort to identify and prevent proximity bias.

Another issue arises in the case of employees who are not exempt from overtime pay requirements. These non-exempt employees (meaning that they must be paid overtime when they work more than a specified number of hours in a workweek) must accurately record and report their time at work, and failing to do so could create an unintended liability for unpaid wages. Another concern with complete flexibility as to when work is performed is even further erosion of the division between work and play (or whatever it is we do when we are not working). Employees who are free to start and stop work not only have to be disciplined to schedule the time they work, but they also need to have a start and end to their workday to avoid the sensation of always being at work.

If leaders are leading, they will be able to identify the employee who is not working. If leaders are leading, they will recognize that some employees work best early or late in the day or will need to step away from their virtual office to address a personal matter. If leaders are leading, they will not require every worker to tell them when they need an hour during the traditional workday for a personal phone call, or to pick a child up from school, or to accompany a family member to a personal appointment. Trust is the key. A good leader will trust employees to do what is expected of them and will be attuned enough to know when an employee is not contributing.

Let's face it: Employees have long worked outside regular business hours and not necessarily during business hours. The recent heightened attention to the idea of a flexible schedule for white-collar workers derives from the 2020–2021 pandemic when workers were glued to their computer all day and all night because there was not much else to do. After months of working without a break, employees began telling their leaders they wanted their lives back.

For those employers who are contemplating a more flexible approach to when work is performed, we recommend two separate policies, one for exempt employees and one for employees who are non-exempt. Given that an organization must track the hours worked by non-exempt employees, this will require that they work a specific schedule, but the organization might provide flexible scheduling for these employees with staggered hours that include workday start and end times before or after traditional business hours. White-collar workers who are non-exempt typically include call center, data entry, and help desk workers as well as administrative workers including assistants and staff in finance or accounting departments.

For exempt employees—leaders, professionals, and high-level individual contributors—organizations generally have no legal obligation to track their hours. In this case, your enterprise should provide business leaders with guardrails and allow leaders to lead in an enlightened way.

THE FLEXIBLE WORKWEEK

What about a shorter workweek? What? Work *less*? Well, why not a shorter workweek? Not just a four-day workweek but a workweek with fewer than 40 hours, or 37.5 hours, or 35 hours (all of which are the typical permutations of a regular workweek). Four-day workweeks are not unusual in some industries. Particularly for some hourly workers such as those in health care (nurses in hospitals) and manufacturing (assembly line work), the four-day workweek has been viewed as a robust alternative. But these four-day workweeks are not about less work; they typically call for four longer workdays of ten or twelve hours rather than eight. These arrangements are sometimes referred to as *compressed* workweeks, meaning that the work typically completed in five days is compressed into fewer days. That's not what we are asking you to consider; we are talking about less work. The newer idea is fewer hours of work while meeting the same productivity expectations.

A bill has been introduced in Congress to amend the Fair Labor Standards Act to provide that overtime compensation begins after 32 and not 40 hours of work each week. While the proposed legislation would not mandate a shorter workweek, it could result in fewer work hours (and most likely lower pay as well). But we predict this type of legislation will go nowhere in the United States—at least not in the near future. But elsewhere in the world, the less-work movement is growing.

Employers in the European Union have experimented with and in some cases adopted shorter workweeks. A detailed report from Iceland identifies many of the benefits associated with a pilot program in which employees in a wide range of jobs moved to a 32-hour and often 4-day workweek. In "Going Public: Iceland's Journey to a Shorter Work Week," the authors describe how businesses were able to accomplish the same (and sometimes a greater) amount of work with fewer hours along with the benefits that employees experienced as a result of working less.[2] How was this accomplished? The report cites shorter meetings, better and increased use of email, cutting unnecessary tasks, improving delegation, reorganizing shifts, taking shorter work breaks, and focusing employees on using days off to accomplish personal errands. Employees who participated in the program reported widespread improvement in their physical and psychological health resulting from less stress and improved morale. Participants in the Iceland study spent more time with their families, had more time for their personal interests, and were just plain happier.

US companies seem to be exploring the idea. Kickstarter and Microsoft received press when they announced pilot programs to institute a shorter workweek yet still provide the same compensation because employees were expected to maintain the same productivity.

What a contrast this is to the reports of the endless work we performed during the worst of the 2020 lockdowns! With little else to do, many white-collar workers just worked for months on end. Yet most of us are much more productive than we were a decade ago because of all the technology that reduces inefficiency. So why are we still working so much? If only we really knew the answer to this question. But the truth is, if we could focus more—meaning not being tempted by household distractions—and use the tools we have to increase productivity effectively, a shorter workweek would be within our reach.

WHO DECIDES

We have begun our discussion of the importance of trust in making a successful transition to a new view of work. Enterprises need to trust that leaders will manage their teams to achieve high levels of productivity yet acknowledge the need for flexibility to retain and attract human capital. Leaders should be vigilant in managing teams whose members may include a distributed workforce and a hybrid workforce. Trust is necessary when managing up (responding to supervision) and managing down (supervising subordinates).

For any hybrid work arrangement to really work, your enterprise must build in opportunities for leaders to be flexible. Equally important is that employees take advantage of the flexibility afforded by a hybrid work policy so that the policy does what it was intended to do, that is, create a design for a positive future of work. Whether your organization implements new approaches as to where work is performed or when work is performed, the changes should offer employees choices. Your hybrid work policy must grant employees some level of control over their work life that enables them to achieve the work–life balance that never existed when they were required to be present in the office all the time.

Employees will want to make decisions so that the benefits of the hybrid policy are tangible. For example, can an employee determine which days he or she must report to the office? When considering a flexible schedule, to what extent can an employee determine whether to start or end a workday early?

Suppose an enterprise has adapted an office-first approach. In conjunction with this approach, the enterprise has created a policy allowing employees to work remotely four days per month but not more than two days in any given week. And the policy requires that a manager approve the designated work-from-home days in advance at the start of every month.

What is lacking in this approach is trust. The point of a hybrid work policy is to provide employees with flexibility. This policy fails to do that. Yes, the employees have the ability to work from home, but they need permission to do so and need to book the days well in advance. That advance notice and limit on when a day can be worked remotely signals something awful to employees: We want to make flexibility as difficult as possible because we don't trust that you will really work when you are not in the office.

With these challenges in mind, to what extent should employees be involved in decision making? Should leaders make decisions for their business units and teams? And once the guardrails are established by an organization's policy, should employees choose the days they work from home? Professor Nicholas Bloom opined in an article for the *Har-*

vard Business Review that employees should not be the ones to decide how often they can work from home. Bloom argued that workers should not set their own work-from-home schedule because "allowing employees to choose their WFH schedule could contribute to a diversity crisis."[3] Just a month earlier, the *Harvard Business Review* published an article by Eric Rosenbaum who cited Harvard Business School Professor Raj Choudhury's admonition that employees and teams should make decisions on remote work and office schedules.[4] So what is the best approach? While Bloom's assessment may be valid, and regardless of whether the enterprise, the business leader, or the employee makes the decision as to how often that employee works away from the office, leaders must affirmatively tackle the potential impact on DEI efforts the hybrid workplace creates.

The social experiment that the pandemic triggered by hastily requiring that massive numbers of white-collar employees work from home accelerated a movement that was already happening. This was the start-up culture movement when offices were outfitted with ping-pong tables and free food was plentiful. According to the start-up culture stereotype, in those free-wheeling office settings employees were free to take advantage of the fun and games during business hours but still got the work done because they worked into the night. The start-up office culture presented an opportunity for employees to have greater freedom in deciding how they worked.

Postpandemic, the focus is not on ways to be free to frolic in the office. The workplace transformation we are now experiencing is to design a positive future of work, one with increased employee freedom to decide where and when to work. The policies we have just discussed do not provide employees with the freedom and flexibility now in demand. The policies are not best in class and will not entice employees to join your organization or to remain.

Now it's time to put pen to paper and draft a policy that meets your organization's needs.

Chapter Two

Codifying Standard Operating Procedures

"Help! We can't get anyone to come back to the office!" Such was the plea from leaders throughout 2021 when they announced initial return-to-work plans. We all read about this phenomenon. First, in the United States, return to work was scheduled for right after key holidays: Memorial Day, then the Fourth of July, then Labor Day, then after Thanksgiving. Some US–based employers tried it this way: By the Fourth of July, everyone is in the office one day each week; by Labor Day up to three days in the office each week; then by Thanksgiving four days in the office each week. Employees vented on social media sites and the press covered the whip-saw pronouncements of our largest corporations. Overall, the plea from employees was "We're remote. It's working, so why change?" Corporate CEOs responded to employee sentiment with every possible response ranging from a hasty withdrawal of the return-to-work proclamation to drawing a line in the sand and insisting on a return to the old way of office every day.

The great RTW (return-to-work) debate has not let up. At the start of 2022, Felice spoke with counsel at a large, multinational employer and learned that this employer had just issued a policy designed to entice reluctant employees back to their offices. Employees at this company were offered an array of benefits if only they would return to the workplace: free lunch, reimbursement of commute costs (parking, public transportation), childcare costs, and even reimbursement of dog walking fees! Just as this company did, many others will demand that their white-collar workforce report to an office—and maybe

offer them perks to do it. In an article in the *New York Times* titled
"Big Tech Makes a Big Bet: Offices Are Still the Future," Kellen
Browning reported that some of the largest tech companies—Meta,
Google, Microsoft, Apple, Salesforce, Amazon, and Twitter—were
expanding the number of offices and the locations of offices throughout the United States and in some instances worldwide.[1] Even Jamie
Dimon, the JP Morgan CEO and diehard proponent of the office-first
approach, finally caved after many public pronouncements that work
must take place in an office. In early April 2022, Dimon's report to
shareholders included a statement that work from home would be "more
permanent in American business." That shareholder report stated 40
percent of JP Morgan's staff would be deemed hybrid and expected to
report to an office a few days a week, with a solid 10 percent designated
as fully remote.[2]

In the face of reluctance, a well-thought-out policy can help.

THE POLICY IMPERATIVE

What is the right approach to where work should be done? It depends on
many factors, which we will get to shortly. If the pandemic triggered your
organization's hasty migration to work from home, it's not surprising that
a leader might think the experience that was forced on many organizations in March 2020 should be viewed as an experiment, and as soon as
it is safe to do so, everyone should go back to where we were in early
March 2020. But the genie was out of the bottle, and white-collar workers
had now had a taste of working away from the office.

Working from home is part of our vernacular and can no longer be
ignored. Hybrid work options are the new norm. Applicants want to
see if the business is remote-first or if it even mentions hybrid work.
At the top of applicants' list of interview questions is "What is the
remote work policy?" They want to know how often they can work
from home or whether they even need to report to an office. Other
applicants wonder if there is an office because they want to see some
colleagues in person at least some of the time. The reality is most
white-collar workers want flexibility as to where they work and when
they work.

So how does this new reality factor into policy making? It means that it is always a good time to step back and consider whether your organization's approach to flexible work is the best one for your organization. Whether your organization has already promulgated a policy answers only part of the question. What matters is not whether your organization has a policy; what matters is whether that policy stands the test of time.

You want a policy that

- reflects your organization's mission and culture
- is fairly administered
- allows your organization to attract the best talent
- contributes to employee retention
- allows your employees to perform their best work
- makes sense; that is, it has requirements based on business needs and doesn't undermine your approach with unjustifiable restrictions that even the most loyal leaders could not readily explain

If the policy is difficult to administer and leaders are forced to make so many exceptions that they out-number the rule, this is a sure sign that the policy is not meeting your organization's needs. Whatever the arrangement, it must make sense. It must be readily understood and support the organization's business goals.

ALIGNING POLICY TO
YOUR ORGANIZATION'S VALUES

A flexible work policy should reflect the organization's mission and values. If the existing policy does not, or if it is not enforced in the manner in which it was intended, then now is the time to start over and recalibrate.

Most organizations will start from an office-first paradigm in evaluating their approach to flexible work because that's where they were before March 2020. Some leaders might think that if the transition to remote work as a result of the pandemic-forced shutdown in 2020 was effective, then their organization should start from the proposition that remote work works. The worldwide health crisis that took us by surprise in 2020 should not frame an organization's decision making. A decision regarding something so critical as where employees will work is too important to be decided on the basis of how well your organization fared during the mandatory work-from-home directives first issued in March 2020. Instead, a clear-headed and strategic review of how work is most successfully performed should be undertaken.

Throughout these chapters you will see key themes repeated. One key theme is remembering your organization's core values. How does a hybrid work policy reflect an organization's core values? Well, for starters, each organization needs a mission statement. Mission statements define corporate culture, values, ethics, and agenda. If your organization is focused on customer service, how can a flexible work policy support excellence in customer service? If your organization is developing artificial intelligence tools and must recruit high-level talent, how does the organization's approach to where work is performed support its ability to attract talent? If your organization supports environmental causes, does a flexible work policy support its environmental mission?

As we address the hybrid work arrangements from which organizations can chose, we urge that the first step in the decision-making process include a discussion of what is really important to the organization. There is no question that collaboration, mentorship, and socialization suffer when all work is performed remotely. It is incredibly difficult to find the organizational glue when all connection is virtual. But as we discuss in the pages that follow, remote work has its advantages: saving commute time, broadening the talent pool, supporting DEI, and even contributing to an organization's environment, society, governance (ESG) goals. Leaders must agree on their organization's values when they begin the task of defining that organization's approach to hybrid work. As the approach to hybrid work is developed, leaders should again review those values to assess whether the decisions made are consistent with those values. By being true to a values perspective, decision making can emerge from the chaos of choice.

As leaders consider their organization's mission and values, they need to answer this question: How do those values translate into flexibility and trust? Think about Patagonia's "Let my people go surfing" approach. What does this say about Patagonia—and how does this approach reflect Patagonia's ethos? We think the approach exactly matches the company's products—outdoor sportswear and equipment—and cultural approach. Why buy these products if you are chained to a desk all day long? If the snow is perfect, grab your Patagonia ski bag and go for it. If the waves are perfect, enjoy them wearing your Patagonia wetsuit.

Chapter Three

Identifying the Best Approach

In May 2021 Felice worked with the executive team of a large employer with headquarters in the New York metropolitan area and satellite offices up and down the East Coast as they debated what approach to take to flexible work. Like that of many employers at the time, their office staff was still largely working from home. Before March 2020, only a handful of the company's employees had done so. The general counsel (GC), chief operating officer (COO), and chief human resources officer (CHRO) were divided. As they hashed out the pros and cons of this issue, what first emerged was their personal bias. The GC loved not having to commute every day and advocated a split-shift approach where employees would be expected to report to their office two or three days each week. The CHRO was remote and did not work in the corporate office in New York. She was uncertain. The COO was in favor of a remote-first approach. They spoke about the chief financial officer (CFO)—not present for the conversation but a key decision maker—who wanted everyone in the office every day.

The individuals were initially focused on advocating their own agenda to preserve and justify their particular preference. They quickly came to realize that their preferences could not be reconciled. All were great promoters of their own agenda!

They then began to share anecdotes that had percolated up from the management team regarding remote experiences during the pandemic. They learned that one remote worker never had an Internet connection at home during the fifteen months this individual was working remotely. "How could that be?" the trio wondered. How did this employee get any work done? Clearly this employee's supervisor was not paying attention and did not even ask the most basic question of the employee, "Do you have an Internet connection?" The three tossed stories back and forth, and all the while their personal interests continued to influence their thinking. As the three leaders hashed out possibilities, they realized that their management team lacked the tools or training to evaluate employee performance away from the office. They realized they could not determine whether the transfer to remote work had been successful. Before taking any steps toward a long-term plan for flexible work arrangements, the leaders came to understand that they must first assess what they had learned from the remote work migration.

As their conversation continued, the leaders came around to understanding that deciding on whether to institute a flexible work policy was a decision of significance. The decision would say a good deal about their organization and could have a significant impact on the future of their organization. Permitting remote work could have multiple benefits. It could

- expand opportunities for recruiting talent
- support caregivers, in particular women
- reduce the need for office space, resulting in savings
- help employees with difficult commutes save money and time

Slowly the leaders put aside their personal agendas and began to explore the range of possibilities.

This employer now offers flexible work to most of its staff, many of who work remotely. As for the accounting team, they're mostly in the office—apparently the CFO got his way.

Every organization will be faced with increasing pressure to consider new, more flexible approaches to where work is performed. Even the most old-fashioned industries and office environments will be faced with pleas from leaders and employees alike to reconsider the office-only choice. Hybrid work in some capacity is the new norm. If your organization or you are not there yet, you will be left behind.

Our advice is this: As your organization approaches policy making, consider all the permutations that are available in the hybrid model.

Put every option on the table as you start the conversation, including options such as

- remote-first
- office-first
- a true hybrid, split-shift mix

Ask yourself if flexibility will be offered to every employee or if the degree of flexibility will depend on the job function. Ask if the policy will address the "when work is performed" question. These are the initial, broad-based choices that must be made. Each organization should make its decision regarding these fundamental questions based on what is right for the organization and its stakeholders and not on whether the organization survived the segue to remote work during the pandemic or as a reaction to the isolation that some employees felt during the pandemic. And as we discuss later, this is a decision that can be fluid. Certainly, leaders should not make a snap decision, because the best way to look at the world of the flexible workplace is by recognizing that a decision made today can and should evolve over time.

WHO SHOULD BE INVOLVED IN DEVELOPING THE FLEXIBLE WORK POLICY?

With the advent of easy-to-use polling, some leaders may feel the pull of letting democracy rule and simply letting staff determine the initial approach. We urge you not to ask your staff to make this decision. You are the leader; take ownership of the decision-making process. What could be more important to the culture of an organization than deciding whether folks work together, side-by-side every day, or whether staff are free to work anywhere in the world? Certainly, employee input is critical. Leaders should listen to what their employees have to say about this very important decision, and as we discuss here, the decision-making team should include a diverse group of voices. Polling, surveys, and roundtables have a place in making and implementing decisions about the hybrid workplace, but asking employees to make the decision will not be helpful in ensuring that the decision making is thoughtful.

Regardless of an organization's current stance on the state of the workplace, deciding where and when work will be performed is a decision that must be made after careful consideration. Reflection is mandatory. The decision should not be based solely on economics or what the competition is doing; the decision should be based on what kind of culture you want to cultivate and to what extent flexible work arrangements will support that culture.

In approaching this exercise, we urge leaders to re-imagine their workplace. Fear of change is understandable. Leaders who are reluctant to change must come to grips with the fact that even the most conservative of industries are changing their outlook toward remote work. This means putting structures in place that ensure that leaders can monitor work performed remotely and stay connected with their teams and stakeholders and that the organization's culture can survive and thrive.

Developing an approach to flexible work requires that leaders be in tune with their workforce. It is rare that members of the C-suite have their ear to the ground and really know what the sentiment of their organization is. For that reason, we urge leaders to consider carefully who will be part of the team that's charged with this task. Here's what we recommend:

- Recognize that representation from human-capital leaders, typically human resources, is necessary.
- Include a sampling of leaders from different divisions, operations, product lines, or geographic areas (for organizations with multiple worksites). Consider identifying not just division heads but a varied group of leaders from different levels.
- Seek diverse voices. Individuals from different generations, long- and short-term leaders, and individuals with different points of reference should be part of the mix. For example, make sure that parents with young children are represented. Women should be included, and the group should have racial diversity. Diverse points of view are critical. The task-force members should bring a variety of biases and viewpoints to the discussion
- Why should leaders hear from employees at the early stages of policy making

A *Future Forum* report found the following:
- 66 percent of executives designed post-pandemic workforce policies with little or no direct employee input
- 66 percent of executives believe they are being "very transparent" regarding post-pandemic policies, while only 42 percent of employees agree
- 44 percent of executives want to work from the office every day, while only 17 percent of employees share this sentiment[1]

What can we learn from this? If decision makers are limited to a group of executives who are the same color, gender, or socio-economic background or have any other circumstantial glue, other voices will never be heard. Executives will be engaging in a process where there are no checks on confirmation bias. Omitting voices that are part of the composition of the staff will undoubtably skew the resulting hybrid work policy. According to the same Future Forum survey, these potentially unheard voices did not echo the same sentiment as corporate leaders. The survey found that Asian, Black, and female respondents favored flexible work arrangements far more than white males, for example.

Most important, before a task force is assembled, leaders must be committed to considering change. If the view from the C-suite is that only employees who don't want to work will choose to work from home, this exercise will not be fruitful. This potential for bias is real. In May 2021, the *New York Times* reported that WeWork's CEO Sandeep Mathrani said that the least-engaged employees are those who enjoy working from home. That statement made headlines. It triggered outrage.

While the task force should include leaders and employees with a variety of points of view and diverse experiences, as part of this reflective exercise, leaders must separate their personal feelings about how they want to work from what will be best for the organization. The members of the task force must be coached to recognize their biases—for example, a baby boomer may resent that employees will now be able to work remotely when he or she commuted (perhaps several hours a day) to an office every day for decades. In the same vein, a leader who is a new parent and wants the flexibility to work remotely to increase the opportunity for family time must set aside personal desire and think instead about the greater good of the organization as flexible work policies are discussed.

Given that personal bias can weigh heavily in evaluating a flexible work policy, a good first step is for the team to be more mindful of their personal biases. Perhaps the decision-making task force should receive anti-bias training before they begin their work. At the very least the team's leader should engage the team in a discussion of how bias can interfere with effective decision making and urge members to identify and interrupt their personal biases. Effective training will set the stage for team members to better identify their personal biases as they begin their discussion. A training session focusing on diversity and inclusion with a curriculum that includes a discussion of confirmation bias, proximity bias, and micro-aggression is a worthwhile investment of the group's time.

The mission of the task force should also be defined. If it is the C-suite's intent to maintain an office-first workplace, provide the task force with that requirement and delegate to the task force the narrower task of developing the core points of a policy that will provide flexibility within the parameters of an office-first workplace. The task force should understand the limitations to its quest. If the organization has made a decision to be office-first or remote-first, the task force must work within the confines of that decision. There is still much to be decided within the confines of a remote-first or office-first approach.

The task force should have a leader or co-leaders, someone to ensure that deadlines are met and that the mission is accomplished. Most important, the leader or co-leaders must be able to manage the process and ensure that the task force sticks to its mission and timetable.

Here is a broad-brush approach to decision making:

- Which positions, if any, are remote-eligible?
- Where will offices be located?
- Which positions that are not designated remote-eligible will be covered by the hybrid work policy?
- What restrictions will apply to those employees who are covered by the hybrid work policy?
- Which positions, if any, will be designated office-only?

Our next chapter will address an approach to address these questions.

Chapter Four

Assessing the Workforce

Those organizations that have decided to embrace hybrid work will likely discuss whether a single approach can be applied to all staff. For organizations embracing hybrid work, the looming question is, Will all employees be expected to report to an office on a regular basis? Before determining whether a one-size-fits-all approach works, we recommend that the team undertake a review of the organization's operations and assess where work needs to be performed. This assessment will vary based on the nature of the business. A technology company may be able to designate all positions remote-first. A retailer could not.

We strongly suggest that if your organization has decided to offer different hybrid options to different groups of employees, the decision should be based on an operational analysis. Policy drafters should be able to explain why some positions are remote-only while others do not have the option of a flexible work arrangement. These are important decisions. Imagine an employee or applicant asks to work remotely and is told that the position is not remote-eligible. When the employee or applicant asks why, the response should make sense. If your organization is going to permit different arrangements for different employees based on business unit, title, or level, those decisions should be made after the organization has undertaken a talent segmentation exercise in which various factors are considered in reaching an understanding as to whether the position is amenable to remote work.

In January 2022 (the Omicron variant of COVID-19 was in the headlines), Felice was working with a financial services group. This

organization maintained several offices of varying size in key metropolitan areas in the United States. The legal team was discussing
various policies, including their flexible work policy. In general
terms, the flexible work policy was a hybrid policy that required most
employees to report to an office on a regular basis—either three or four
days a week depending on the business unit. But the group had also
determined that up to 5 percent of the workforce would be permitted to
work remotely anywhere in the country. When Felice asked how that
5 percent was determined, she learned that the opportunity to work remotely was on a first-come-first-served basis. This policy was already
having troubling repercussions. First, it was becoming increasingly difficult to navigate the legal landscape when employees worked remotely
in so many states. Second, it was becoming impossible for leadership to
explain why 5 percent was reasonable. Finally, many of the employees
who had been given the opportunity to be remote were in positions that
were not the best suited for remote work.

As we discuss in section IV, where an employee works typically
determines which state and local laws govern that employee—
for example, laws that govern payments to state unemployment funds
and paid leave funds or compliance with workers compensation laws
and withholding and remitting taxes to states and sometimes localities. Further, laws regarding pay, leave, and restrictive covenant laws
(laws that address whether an employer can restrict an employee from
competing or soliciting customers, for example) are typically based on
where the employee is working. That 5 percent of the workforce was
located in about twenty-five states, making compliance with workplace
laws more complicated than the organization had anticipated.

The second issue that quickly percolated from staff was related to
the process by which employees were awarded the right to work remotely. The organization was now facing inquiries from employees
who had missed the chance to apply for the right to work remotely.
These employees were complaining that the 5 percent figure was too
low and had been arbitrarily set. Employees who wanted the ability to
work remotely argued that more employees should have the opportunity
to work remotely. Faced with these issues, Felice and the leaders discussed whether it would have made more sense to approach the decision
of who should work remotely a bit differently. There was no basis for
the 5 percent figure. It was arbitrary and intended to allow some remote

work but not too much remote work. And in awarding the remote designation, the organization had not considered whether the individuals who asked for permission first held positions where their remote status would impact their ability to perform or whether this remote status would negatively impact the employee's business unit's performance. But it seemed too late to revisit this issue. Or was it?

Had the organization's leaders considered a more rational basis for identifying which positions should be designated remote based on the individual's function, the decision making would have stood up to the scrutiny of employees who asked, "Why can't I work remotely?" When the leaders were faced with employees asking, "Why can't 10 or even 15 percent of the workforce work remotely when we've all been remote for more than two years?", they did not have a good answer. It is never a good moment for an organization when leaders cannot comfortably and sincerely answer questions about a policy they've created.

As we present a way forward—an approach to devising a hybrid policy—our goal is for your organization to avoid many of these issues. The financial services company's plan to designate 5 percent of the staff was well intentioned. At the time the initial program was implemented, 5 percent seemed generous, and the organization's leaders thought that would meet the need to retain talent that had relocated around the country during the 2020 pandemic while providing an adequate opportunity to recruit hard-to-find talent. The spirit of the policy was positive. But the potential impact of this random choice surfaced. Even so it was not too late to fix the problem before it created a human resources issue and impacted morale or, worse yet, led to employee defections.

This case study demonstrates the importance of including varied voices in your task force. Intentionality must reign throughout this process. Who was part of the financial services organization's decision-making team? Whoever it was, that group did not have an accurate reading of employee sentiment. The folks who came up with the 5 percent approach were in a bubble. They thought their policy would demonstrate forward thinking and generosity. Instead, it fell flat and did not begin to meet the demands of the workforce.

As the organization's leaders began to hear the rumblings of employee discontent, they came to understand how difficult it would be to administer the policy they'd created. They decided to recalibrate. It was not too late to change; it's never too late to change.

The organization was quick to pivot. The percentage would be lifted. And instead of enforcing a completely random selection of remote-eligible positions, the organization undertook a strategic review of its business model and identified those functions that could best be performed remotely and those functions that would be designated office-first and eligible for split-shift arrangements. The organization also faced the realization that its efforts to limit the number of states in which its remote employees worked was not feasible. Long term, they did not want their recruitment efforts to be limited to only a certain number of states, meaning that once they designated a position remote-eligible, it did not matter where in the United States the employee lived.

We anticipate that many, many organizations will make the decision to designate some number of their staff remote. For organizations that seek to develop a hybrid policy such that some number of employees regularly report to an office, the decision as to which team members may work remotely should be among the first decisions made. How to determine which positions to identify as remote-eligible? We suggest a talent segmentation exercise.

TALENT SEGMENTATION

Segmentation typically involves identifying groups of employees based on a hierarchical or compensation basis or job cluster or business unit basis. In the past decade, employers have relied on segmentation to better align benefits and develop talent programs. Employee segmentation began as an outgrowth of marketing segmentation. The same benefits companies can achieve from better understanding distinct markets can be used in the human capital arena. Understanding the needs of employee segments has emerged as a tool for human capital experts to better assess the needs and desires of particular groups of employees.[1] The talent segmentation we contemplate in connection with preparing a flexible work policy requires a deeper look at employee skills and what skills are needed to achieve what is expected from a job. By understanding how particular groups of employees work, your organization will be better equipped to determine whether specific work can be performed away from an office and coworkers all of the time, some of the time, or never. This essentially calls for a strategic and introspective process.

We propose that such an exercise is helpful in identifying the function of employees who can work remotely and those functions where employees will not be able to reach the highest level of performance without some regular opportunity to work in person with colleagues.

A segmenting analysis can also assist leaders by providing a way to determine whether a flexible work policy can be applied to all employees or just a portion of the employee complement. Undertaking a segmentation exercise can be very helpful to organizations that aspire to be remote-first but want to be certain that if there are clusters of business functions where in-person meetings enhance performance, the organization does not overlook this need. Likewise, for organizations determined to maintain an office-first approach but wanting to secure the benefits of a distributed workforce, knowing which positions may be designated remote without compromising collaboration will provide needed direction in making decisions about flexible work programs. Understanding the skills needed for segments of a workforce has long been recognized as a way for organizations to customize total rewards programs so as to have the greatest impact on attracting and retaining talent. We suggest a similar review will help your organization recognize where and when work can be performed, thus informing flexible work policies.

The segmenting exercise allows your organization to align talent models with business strategy. A careful look at how work is performed in specific business units will help leaders understand whether a one-size-fits-all approach to flexible work will meet their organization's needs. Organizations often rely on consultants to conduct a segmentation analysis, but the project can be completed in house. Our suggestions below will help your organization begin the process. The purpose of the segmenting exercise is to objectively determine which positions can be performed well remotely, which are best performed on a hybrid work schedule, and which positions must be performed exclusively in an office. By undertaking a fact-based inquiry that focuses on the work itself, your organization's leaders will be able to credibly explain their approach to where work must be performed. The following are basic questions that should be answered as part of this segmenting inquiry.

- Which functions or teams were most readily transferred away from a physical office and achieved excellence? Why were those functions or teams successful? For employees who did not meet goals in these positions, what were the roadblocks? Could these roadblocks have been addressed by the organization?
- Which positions require in-person mentoring—the opportunity to watch and listen to more experienced team members as a critical part of training and skills development? Can that in-person mentoring be assured within the remote work model or is in-person training necessary?
- Which leaders were able to maintain connections with their staff and ensure that the interpersonal glue was strong? What strategies did those leaders use to bond and mentor remote staff? Can these strategies for success be taught to and adopted by other leaders who supervise employees who perform different types of work?
- Which positions require a wide geographic net from which to recruit talent?

Flexible work arrangements should help employers achieve best-in-class status by attracting and retaining talent, not the contrary. As leaders review the results of a segmenting exercise, they should review whether the implications for recruiting and retaining talent meet your organization's needs. For example, if your organization has a need for talent that cannot uniformly be met in the marketplaces where the organization maintains offices, then your organization will need to expand the scope of its remote workforce.

Once the organization has identified remote-eligible positions, a process should be in place to address questions about and requests for policy exceptions. Anticipate that there will be employees who are not in remote-eligible positions who want to be considered for remote status. A team—perhaps lead by the organization's human capital or people team—should be in place to review requests for exceptions to the policy (this is different from situations where employees request remote status as an accommodation based on disability, for example; more on this later). Why some positions may be worked remotely and others may not will be challenged by employees, so leaders should be ready to address these questions as they arise.

Human capital leaders also should anticipate that as their organization grows and identifies new positions, an evaluation will be made before recruiting activities begin to determine whether this new position will be remote-eligible. An evaluative tool will help organizations as they develop new positions. Segmentation analysis will lead to the creation of this evaluative tool.

THE SPLIT-SHIFT WORK SCHEDULE

So many choices. Three days in the office, two days remote each week? A minimum of two days in the office per week? One week in the office per month? Should the days be mandated? Will employees and team leaders have the flexibility to decide which days are remote? The permutations are endless.

Our suggestion on where to begin is this: Review your organization's value statement. Remember that introduction that is on the virtual white board? Read it. What is the purpose of the hybrid approach? What are the goals that your organization wishes to achieve by instituting flexibility in where work is performed?

The first step of this scheduling assessment is to determine why employees are required to work in an office some of the time. Is it to meet with one another to engage in creative thinking? Is it to provide mentorship for new members of the organization or those who are developing skills? Is it to develop community? Remember: You will need to communicate to your organization's employees the rationale behind your decision. Be prepared to deliver the why.

When we discuss communicating a policy, we suggest that the policy include an introduction to serve as the underlying basis for all these decisions. That introduction is the organization's value statement and will always serve as a guide for every one of these decisions. That statement may be the introduction the task force has already prepared that is on the virtual white board staring at the task force each time it meets. If the task force drafts the introduction at the start of the decision-making process, this will not only serve as a guiding principle, it will answer all the questions employees (and applicants) may ask about the rationale behind the policy. Keeping this introduction on the virtual white board as the task force works through the process will keep the task force honest to its mission.

The first of the big questions is, How often will employees report to an office? Here are the basic possibilities, with considerations about in-office accommodations to follow.

- without a set schedule, at the discretion of the employee—e.g., Come to the office as often as you like.
- without a set schedule, at the discretion of the employee, except when there is a specific requirement—e.g., Come to the office as often as you like, but when your manager asks you to report in person, we expect you to be there.
- with a set minimum with no particular schedule—e.g., We expect to see you two days a week, you decide when.
- with a set minimum with a designated schedule—e.g., We expect to see you three days a week, and your team's days in the office are Monday to Wednesday.

The schedule must align with your organization's real estate, of course. Driving at least in part the options you offer are space—not just room for everyone but collaborative spaces—for all employees to report to the office when they are expected to be there. This is an important consideration, because organizations that embrace flexible work arrangements will undoubtably want to reap the economic benefit (and the possible positive environmental impact) of a reduced real estate footprint.

In deciding upon the terms of the hybrid schedule, the task force should consider the following:

- Will new employees, or those filling positions that require a high level of mentorship because they are in training positions or positions where skills development are key, be required to be present in an office to ensure supervision and support? If so, for how long? If mentees are required to be present in an office, will the program provide for mentors to be present in a meaningful way?
- Can attendance in the office be coordinated so that the desired collaboration, synergy, and socialization actually take place?

Let's take each one of these questions in turn. The task force should discuss whether new hires, trainees, and those employees in entry-level positions should be addressed separately in the policy. Will these employees benefit from an increased obligation to report to an office? What will these individuals miss out on if they are not physically present? Contemplate this question well because there is no one-size-fits-all answer. Keep in mind that requiring some staff to report to the office so that they can learn from more experienced colleagues only works when the more experienced colleagues are in the office. Team leaders and mentors will need to buy in to this commitment. Requiring developing talent to report to an office only to spend their day in meetings on virtual platforms does not provide the teachable moments that in-person collaboration is intended to create.

Next is the question of how often employees must be in the office and who gets to decide the particulars as to when. Let's dissect the underlying goals of in-person interaction. From that discussion, leaders will be in a position to better evaluate which tasks must be performed in person and which tasks do not require in-person engagement. Employees who are provided with choices as to when and how much time to spend in person with colleagues and leaders will be in a position to maximize their learning and collaborative experiences and make better decisions about when and for what purpose office work is best.

We recommend that your enterprise set the policy and leave day-to-day administration to its leaders. The enterprise should determine the extent of each individual's minimum on-site commitment, which will typically be based on their role. If days in an office are mandated, it makes sense that employees who work together should all be present in their office together some of the time. We discuss this in our next chapters, but let's set the stage for this discussion now. If your organization is instituting a hybrid approach and requires employees to report to an office some of the time, your leaders must make sure that the time in the office is meaningful. What good is reporting to an office if no one else from your team is present on the same day? Ideally, your leaders will schedule collaborative sessions when their team members are present so that time in the office is used wisely. We recommend that leaders do the following to facilitate collaboration.

- Designate the days each week when all team members should be present. Certainly this should be done with staff input.
- Ensure leaders are present and rotate their days in the office to ensure that they have in-person contact with every team member. And when they are present, leaders should be engaging with every team member. Leaders must be held accountable for ensuring that they make the most out of their contributors' time in the office.

Again, while the enterprise should issue the policy, business leaders should be vested with the ability to manage their departments and teams.

THE "WHEN" OF WORK

You've succeeded! The task force has now

- decided which positions are remote-eligible
- determined the schedule if any, for the hybrid employee complement
- identified who will decide the parameters of the split-shift schedule

But the task force is not yet done. Remember the *when* question we discussed in chapter 1? Now is the time for your organization to articulate a further viewpoint regarding flexibility.

Again, we cannot offer your organization a best approach because every organization will have a personalized value statement and operational challenges. For example, at one end of the spectrum might be a team of call center employees or IT help desk assistants. These individuals are focused on meeting customer service goals, and their organization must ensure that there is adequate staffing to respond to in-the-moment requests. Fixed schedules are a must for these white-collar workers. But how about marketing professionals? Do they need to adhere to a 9 to 5 Monday to Friday schedule? Probably not. For these individuals, flexibility as to when work is performed is certainly a possibility. As long as these individuals attend necessary meetings and are available to answer time-sensitive inquiries, their work can be performed at any time.

Flexible work hours may be the de facto arrangement in your organization, meaning this is what happens but is not officially sanctioned. If that's the case, then better to sanction the arrangement and reap the benefit of promoting a more flexible approach to work! Also, it's better to make clear which positions are not permitted to deviate from a set schedule. Not only are customer service teams likely relegated to a fixed schedule, but white-collar employees who are not exempt from the overtime pay requirements set by federal and state laws should also have a fixed schedule. When organizations fail to limit and track the time that hourly employees work, the unintended consequences may be additional pay obligations.

The best approach? Your organization should train leaders to understand which of their direct reports are able to work flexibly.

Chapter Five

Drafting and Communicating the Policy

At the start of 2022, we spoke with a human capital leader employed by a large private university. Once the university's students returned to campus after the pandemic shutdowns, the university issued a policy that gave deans the ability to determine which positions could be designated remote or hybrid-based on the individual dean's assessment as to whether working away from campus detrimentally impacted the student community. As for the hybrid designation, deans were free to set rules as to the various hybrid schedules. This approach provided deans with flexibility but resulted in inconsistent approaches depending on a particular dean's view of the work performed and its connection to student engagement. The result was lots of resignations, which might have been inevitable given the breadth of the great resignation movement but also could have been prompted by employee discontent with the outcomes of these determinations. Lesson to be learned? A policy needs guardrails to ensure that employees see its outcomes as fair and reasonable. Too much flexibility can be just as detrimental as an inflexible approach.

Policy drafting requires organization and precision. Leaders, do not rush this part. If your task force has considered and answered all the questions that we've outlined thus far, the policy should be easy to write because the answers to the basic questions have all been answered in the decision-making process. But even if the protocols are clear to the task force, sloppy, ill-conceived writing will come back to haunt your organization. In addition to the policy, the organization should prepare an entire communications playbook, including FAQs and training modules.

In addition, the policy should be referenced in employee handbooks, offer letters, and employment agreements. Most important, the policy should be clear. An employee should be able to understand the policy after one reading.

Here are our basic tips for the policy drafting proces:

1. State the purpose of the policy. Integrate your organization's value statement and purpose. For example, if your organization has chosen an office-first approach with a robust hybrid option allowing employees to work away from the office several days each week, explain why the organization supports flexibility.
2. Make sure key terms are defined. Don't assume that every reader has the same understanding as to the meaning of buzz words. Start with *remote* and *hybrid* and move on to what it means to have a *collaborative office day*. A glossary at the end of the policy is a good approach.
3. Specify what the new policy is. This is where the various components are set out.
4. Explain any processes required by the policy. This is where implementation is discussed.
5. Identify a point person for implementation and to whom questions should be addressed.
6. Include protocols for accommodation requests. Identify a process for redress or questions.
7. Specify when the policy will be effective.

Here are some questions that should be clearly answered by your split-shift hybrid work policy.

- What is the process by which it is decided what days particular employees should be in the office?
- Will the enterprise mandate particular days when all employees must report to work?
- Will employees have the option to work in the office more frequently than the minimum requirement?
- If employees can choose their days in the office, how will this be communicated to leaders who will want some in-person contact with all their team members?

It should not be difficult for a leader to check compliance with the minimum in-person requirements. Enterprises should not just confirm that employees are reporting for work in-person on a regular basis but also should be assessing whether all business units permit the remote work and support the truly hybrid arrangement that a split-shift policy affords. If there are leaders who require their staff to report live and do not take advantage of the split-shift policy, your enterprise should be aware of this so that the leader is reminded that the policy is available to all staff.

How much detail should be in the policy? Just enough. There is no need to list the positions that are remote-eligible. The policy should make it clear that employees who hold remote-eligible positions will be advised by their business leader or the human capital team. Does the policy need to state the split-shift schedules of all employees? No again. The policy need only state that each business leader will communicate the available split-shift arrangements to their team. If it is necessary to book a spot in the office, the policy should so state that arrangements must be made and perhaps refer to a scheduling policy that outlines the details regarding booking a workspace. But the policy should state that employees with a split shift are expected to adhere to it and should explain why reporting to an office as required by the split shift is necessary.

For those organizations that have elected an office-first approach but will provide employees with the ability to work remotely on occasion and are not ready to embrace split-shift arrangements, the task force should ensure that the policy is focused on the flexibility that the policy is intended to provide. If the organization is providing employees with the ability to work from home sometimes, do not encumber the process so as to eliminate its impact! Make sure the policy responds to employee demand for flexibility by not requiring employees to jump through hoops to schedule remote days off. With these goals in mind, a policy that severely limits the days of the week employees can designate remote workdays requires excessive advance notice when an employee wishes to designate a day as a remote workday, or grants managers broad discretion to deny requests to work remotely obstructs your goal of providing white-collar workers with a benefit.

Once your enterprise issues the policy, leaders should be provided with direction and granted the ability to manage their businesses.

Administering a hybrid work policy should not become a daily burden or a cause for continuous negotiation and strife. Here's where trust between the enterprise, the leader, and the employee must exist. Without trust a leader might micromanage the way in which every employee adheres to the remote-work policy. The enterprise must train (and trust) leaders to apply the policy in an even handed and just way.

As organizations with office-first policies increasingly adopt more-flexible arrangements, they will be faced with requests from employees and leaders alike to expand (and limit) these arrangements. How should leaders respond to requests to broaden the rules that have been published after much debate and consideration? In some circumstances, leaders will have a legal obligation to accommodate requests to broaden their remote work policy (discussed later in section IV). When employees present a medical condition or disability and request to be designated a remote employee or ask to have the flexibility of scheduling more remote workdays than provided for by the policy, your enterprise may have a legal obligation to provide an accommodation that addresses the employee's need for greater flexibility. But there may be other reasons leaders should entertain requests. We encourage leaders to listen.

Those remote workers employed by an office-first employer have unique challenges. Succeeding while working remotely when most employees report to an office requires an intentional effort to engage. We offer suggestions to remote workers who constitute a minority in our discussion of the organizational glue and the 7 *C*s in section II. In short, remote workers must learn to engage with their colleagues, who may view them as out of sight, out of mind.

STAKEHOLDER SUPPORT

The task force has completed its work. The policy is written. It's time to report to the C-suite and others, who will weigh in. The task force needs to be sure that leaders understand the goals of the policy and how the process will work. More important, stakeholders need to support the policy. The business leadership needs to be sure that the task force has not missed an important issue and has considered the likely questions that may arise. Convincing leaders to support change may or may not be a challenge to your organization. Depending on the organization's culture, it may be necessary to provide leaders with an opportunity to do more than just implement the policy; it may be necessary to provide leaders with an opportunity to weigh in. If so, tread carefully. If your task force has done its work, stakeholders should not be able to turn the policy upside down.

The leadership team must be aligned when the hybrid work approach is communicated. If the organization decides to embrace a split-schedule approach, but a division leader—someone with clout—refuses to embrace the decision and his team knows they are expected in the workplace every day, this situation should be addressed from the start. Is it the leader's cult of personality that is the reason this leader believes an office-focused environment is necessary? Or is it that the work being done by the division really lends itself to in-person collaboration on a regular basis? Our advice to leaders is to be confident that leadership is unified in their support before the communications campaign begins. If that requires different rules for different divisions or locations, that may be the best outcome. The best decision is one that allows employees to be as successful as possible. If the barrier to change is an executive who is inflexible, then that issue must be addressed before your organization announces and implements its decision. No leader should be in a position to undermine this decision.

COMMUNICATIONS CAMPAIGN

An effective communications plan is key. A timeline with cascading communications, FAQs, training, and an opportunity to ask questions are all important components of an effective campaign. A remote work policy is more than just a human resources policy, it is a reflection of your organization's values and says *everything* about the organization. There can never be too much planning. Communicating the plan is not exclusively the job of the human capital team. Operations leaders should have an outsized role in the communications plan, and they should be part of the communications rollout. Your organization's marketing team should apply its skills to this process.

The focus group or pilot program should have addressed the written communications. At the point of announcing the policy, your leaders should be confident that the FAQs address the likely questions. Those individuals who are assigned responsibility for addressing concerns should be trained and prepared and ready to address issues in a consistent fashion.

Here are some key pointers:

- Will there be a notice period before employees are required to report to an office? Consider how much notice is reasonable when employees need to rejigger their lives, whether it is finding childcare or buying a vehicle to commute to work.
- Anticipate which employees will feel the change the most. Make certain this group's leaders are prepared to address their concerns.
- See to it that your public relations team is at the ready and involved in the announcement. Depending on your organizations size and the change in policy, the new policy may be worthy of publicity. At the very least, social media and other outlets should be engaged.

RECALIBRATION

The task of assessing and then re-assessing your organization's remote work policy is one that leaders of the future will need to regularly contend with. As the state of connectivity in the United States improves with the expansion of broadband, leaders will be faced with increasing opportunities to expand their approach to the hybrid workplace. Employee migration to more remote locations and away from city centers will continue, putting increasing pressure on leaders to reconsider and adapt to the use of more flexible approaches to a remote work policy. Undoubtably there will be a need to recalibrate remote work policies from time to time. Leaders must have their ear to the ground and listen and learn from each hybrid experience.

How often should leaders undertake a workplace re-assessment? That depends. But some subset of the task force may be the right team to regroup on a regular basis to evaluate how the policy is working and whether it is meeting its goals.

Various circumstances may trigger a recalibration:

1. The expiration of a significant lease for office space.
2. Growth in new locations and the need to consider expanding to new office space.
3. Changes in the ability to recruit, attract, or retain employees.

4. A need to scale up (or down).
5. Feedback from employees and leaders that the current model is losing its effectiveness.
6. Increased requests from employees for exceptions to the existing policy.

CONSISTENT POLICIES

- Employment documents, offer letters, and contracts need to be consistent.
- See to it that job postings are updated based on the new hybrid policy. In addition, offer letters, employment contracts, and employment documents should specify the work environment or office location from which the employee will work. When you're transitioning to a hybrid work environment, these documents must be updated to reflect the new work model. Likewise, employee handbooks should be updated to reflect your organization's guidelines for hybrid or remote work and ensure that they set the appropriate expectations and rules for privacy, confidentiality, and data protection.

Section II

THE 7 Cs OF LEADERSHIP

The 7 Cs light the path forward in refining and implementing your hybrid work policy. They focus on the steps to become an inspirational leader and build interpersonal glue among your employees, whether they see each other face to face regularly, occasionally, or perhaps only virtually. That includes learning the multifaceted parts of leadership, building connections with individual team members, and facilitating connections among them.

The 7 Cs are culture, change, connection, communication, collaboration, compassion, and coaching.

Chapter Six

Culture

As Francis Frei and Anne Morriss said, "If we may be blunt for a second, what the hell is *culture*?"[1] They have spent years at Harvard and the Leadership Consortium defining *culture*. It is a complex and somewhat amorphous concept. After much research, they assert that there are three components of good cultures: clarity, communication, and consistency. Here is one of their attempts to offer a starting point: "Culture tells us what to do when the CEO isn't in the room, which of course is most of the time." But who is ultimately responsible for clarity, communication, and consistency and is in the room most of the time? Leaders are.

After a large-scale re-organization at a large media and entertainment company, Anna, EVP (Executive Vice President) of the press department, wanted to integrate a newly formed team. The new team was the result of merging six channels (including many of the shows that you have probably binge watched) into one large press department. Anna celebrated the diversity within the newly formed department. She wanted to provide clarity and communicate her values and working principles to create a supportive culture with high standards, so she reached out to Julie to facilitate a three-day team-building offsite. Anna opened with her State of the Department speech. She described her worker-first approach to maximizing productivity. The purpose of the offsite was to build new processes and interpersonal glue. Her values included things such as "producing high-quality work that can be done anywhere" (that is, office versus home was up to everyone), answering emails in a timely way, and providing a budget for social events. She modeled building interpersonal glue by sharing some personal things about her family and her life outside of work.

Three days of concentrated work followed: clarifying jobs, developing guidelines for who does what, getting to know each other, and having just plain fun. The last day of the offsite was a Friday. It was a beautiful day. Anna began the day with a message to the team: "We'll end after lunch today. I encourage you to finish your work as soon as possible and take the afternoon off."

The following Monday morning, Julie met with Chris, a senior leader at a different company. He began the meeting with complaining that no one was in the office on Friday afternoon and emails were not getting returned.

Which leader would you rather work for? Anna or Chris?

Chris wanted to maximize productivity. However, he failed to appreciate that productivity requires a team that feels respected, understands the bigger picture, and is committed to meeting deliverables. Anna wanted to create a culture that ensured engagement and well-being for her team in addition to maximizing productivity. She was clear about her values. She communicated them and set the team up for success by getting them to clarify details that were necessary to maintain consistency in living the values. Anna recognized the importance in a hybrid world of strengthening the bonds among the team. She prioritized getting her team together to break bread together literally and figuratively. Hence, months ago she budgeted money to facilitate connections to drive the organizational change.

Anna is an inspirational leader. To create an engaged and highly productive team, she lived the 7 Cs: culture, change, connection, communication, collaboration, compassion, and coaching.

After the enterprise designs the hybrid workplace, the next step is ensuring the culture changes align with the new mission, values, and guidelines. The baton gets passed from the enterprise to the leaders to individual team members who need to change and live it.

A technology client of Julie's had a mission that included the value of bringing your whole self to work. Leaders were encouraged to bring "non-work parts of their lives" into their work. A couple of team members loved dogs. In six months, Buster, a friendly chocolate Labrador retriever, roamed the halls of their office with ease. Another team was full of working parents. Many had kids who met their coworkers via Zoom as they walked into their parents' home office during a virtual meeting. The team opted to have a monthly Bring Your Kids to Work

Day on the last Friday afternoon of every month. Who doesn't get energized around kids' smiles and energy? (We'll grant you, cranky teenagers bring different energy.) The team got as much out of the visits as the children did. In contrast, leaders who do not connect their behavior with the organization's mission and values get labeled "bad bosses." One bad boss was a client with a mission to create a "company that respected boundaries." A boss sending emails twenty-four hours per day, seven days a week was not living a company value. Just like Chris, she had a disgruntled team with low productivity. Culture starts with defining then sharing your company's vision and values.

DEFINING YOUR VALUE PROPOSITION

Defining and sharing your values and mission is a crucial step in building a successful hybrid culture. Even more important than offering employees flexible, hybrid work arrangements is employees feeling aligned and connected to your vision. For example, a 2009 study published in the *Journal of Marketing* asserted with no caveats that "corporate culture is the strongest driver of radical innovation."[2]

Corporate culture matters 10 to 20 percent more than the ability to work from home and hybrid work availability.[3] In order to further operationalize your vision and values as they are the bedrock of your company, think about what you would like leaders to do and employees to say about your company. People may not say, "This is our culture" or "This is our value proposition," but they will say things that matter to them. Here are some examples of what employees may say in a company that lives its values.

Value proposition: **Create a learning environment**. Leaders may discuss learning opportunities with their team. Employee says, "The company provides stipends for each employee."

Value proposition: **Respect personal boundaries**. Leaders may work during normal business hours and expect team to do the same. Employee says, "My boss doesn't email me after 7 p.m. or on weekends."

Value proposition: **Empower employees**. Leaders may give work to their team and expect them to meet deliverables on their own. Employee says, "I can decide which theme to use for the website design."

Value proposition: **Take safe risks**. Leaders may give stretch projects to their team. Employee says, "I made a mistake last week on the new project. My boss didn't criticize me. He taught me how to do it better next time." Of note, a well-known Google study found that being able to take safe risks was one of key components of highly functioning teams.[4]

Value proposition: **Share the vision**. Leaders may have regular update meetings with the entire team. Employee says, "We have team-wide meetings so everyone knows what everyone is working on."

Value proposition: **Collaborate across location**. Leaders may budget for new technology. Employee says, "Our conference rooms now have bigger monitors. Now we can see expressions on the faces of people working from home."

TRUST

While bigger monitors can help teammates see each other better in team meetings, much of the work that people do cannot be seen. Trust, or lack of trust, can be felt in many ways. Surveilling employees, whether using stealth software, expecting face time for the sake of face time, literally looking over someone's shoulder, or reaching out to an employee to test his or her responsiveness may decrease productivity and morale. Trust doesn't entail having no expectations of your team. It's hard to measure if someone is working. Does sitting at your computer constitute work? Does providing instant responses to emails, even if they're incorrect, constitute work? Trust entails holding your team accountable for their work and meeting deliverables. When you expect others to be accountable, you are also communicating that you value them and their contributions to the team. Trust is a two-way street. You expect them to be accountable, they need to deliver. According to Paul J. Zak, founder of the Center for Neuroeconomics Studies and author of *Trust Factor: The Science of Creating High-Performance Companies*, employees with high trust for their organization feel 74 percent less stressed and 50 percent more productive.[5]

Ask yourself, what is driving your distrust? Is it your beliefs about hybrid work? Perhaps you are resistant to change? Perhaps you like going to the office five days a week and want to see your team five days per week?

Rather than starting with "Trust has to be earned," start with trusting your team until they violate that trust. It is reasonable for managers to expect employees to be reliable. Employees demonstrate they are trustworthy by, first and foremost, meeting their deliverables. If an employee's assignment is to meet you in Washington with a client's report, it's okay if the person takes a plane, train, car, or even a bike if they're on time and within budget. Oh, and they confirmed that you're in Washington State, and not Washington, DC.

Shift from "Here's the work that has to get done" to "Here are the outcomes we want."

Just as we recommend you say as you do and do as you say, it's reasonable to expect follow through with commitments. Commitments include following a hybrid schedule, communicating with the team, arriving on time, being engaged in meetings, and responding in a timely manner. *Timely* is a "big word" that different people interpret differently. *Timely* may mean responding within twenty-four hours, or *timely* may mean responding within an hour. We suggest you replace the word *timely* with a number or time.

If there are gaps between expectations and behavior, chances are it is not because someone is lazy or trying to get away with something. Rather, it's a breakdown in communication.

WORK–LIFE BALANCE

When someone is asked if his or her company has a good culture, chances are the initial response will be about work–life balance—or lack thereof. We don't know about you, but we've never met anyone who works eighty-plus hours a week and says his or her company has a respectful, positive culture. If a team member tells you he or she want to discuss work–life balance, it may be code for "I don't want to work past 6:00 p.m. or respond to emails over the weekend." So too with trust, it may not be the person is lazy. It may be the person has too much work for one person or may need help setting boundaries. The manager's response to any concern about work–life balance is what will impact the culture of the department. In a large study, Gallup found that manager's responses to employees accounted for 70 percent of the employee's engagement.[6]

Consider your role as a manager. Do you model balance and boundaries? Do you expect your team to always think about work, perhaps just like you? That may work for you, but it won't for many employees. Most people need boundaries to maintain mental and physical health. Members of your team may need help creating boundaries for when and where they are connected with work to avoid burnout.

Arianna Huffington, founder of Thrive Global, suggests *work–life balance* may be a misnomer. Rather *life–work integration* is a more accurate framework for leaders to consider when creating a positive culture.[7] As we stated at the beginning of this book, the idea of separate worlds is a myth. Living and working coexist for all of us. Concepts such as "Bring your whole self to work" highlight the need for integration. The challenge for organizations is creating a culture that helps employees align their values with how they are spending their time.

Work–life balance may also be code for desiring a sense of fulfillment and contentment. Organizations that maintain a culture maximizing employee satisfaction and engagement, combined with leaders who care, will have engaged, happy, committed employees. Caring leaders require empathy and compassion (read on).

CONNECTION

Culture begins and ends with the people. You walk into any building, and something always happens. Consider how many "This guy walks into a bar" jokes there are. Something always happens. So too, every time you walk into your office building, something happens. You connect with the company you work for. When you walk into your office, you connect with the people you work with. Connecting with your company and coworkers is essential to maintain a successful organization.

When employees work full-time in the office, the daily connection is maintained: with their company. With their coworkers. You may or may not have enjoyed your commute. But either way, once you're there it feels good. Seeing people. Smiles. You can catch Joe to ask him a quick question. You can drop by your boss's office to hear her reactions to the report you sent yesterday. You can stop by the kitchen just to see who is around. It feels good.

In contrast to the everyday ritual of walking into the office, during 2020 when much of the world was shut down, the ritual of walking into the office didn't occur. We lost connections to our respective companies. People became disengaged and were alone. There was no glue keeping the culture alive.

It became a perfect storm. No connection to the company. It was hard to connect with others. Unhappy and burnt out. There was diminished or no loyalty. For many, it became easier to quit. You didn't even have to have an awkward conversation with your boss or go to HR. You could send a two-word text: "I quit." So many people did this that what ended up happening became known as the Great Resignation. People quit when they don't have loyalty to their job. The reverse of it is a culture that fosters connections and creates loyal employees.

GROWTH AND DEVELOPMENT

Keeping up with our changing world requires organizational cultures with a growth mindset. A growth mindset that is shared by the enterprise and supported as a component of employee development will drive organizational success. In her 2007 book *Mindset: The New Psychology of Success*, psychologist Carol Dweck coined the term "growth mindset," or the ability to learn and change, by contrasting it with the "fixed mindset" of those who think they can't.[8] Cultures need to go beyond defining themselves as learning organizations if they want to grow as a business and keep loyal employees. Research has shown that when most employees feel they have opportunities to learn and grow at work, there is a noticeable uptick in productivity and significant decrease in absenteeism.

Resources are needed such as training and development departments that focus on individual and team growth, managers who take time to coach employees, leaders who facilitate teams, leaders who earmark funds for individual education, and motivated employees who want to learn. Having managers who take an interest in and support an employee's development is a straight route to loyalty. Companies with growth cultures will not only be competitive in the market, they'll attract talent. The second question an applicant will ask is, "What are the opportunities for growth and advancement?" The first is, "What is your hybrid policy?

CARING

People want to work with others who care. Creating a caring culture may sound simplistic, but it isn't. It has different meanings in different companies. Like all the other components of culture, declaring in a mission statement that you have a respectful and supportive culture isn't enough. Reflect on the words that embody what caring looks like for your culture. There may be more than one: *kind, respectful, thoughtful, understanding, considerate, generous, supportive, empathetic, charitable, compassionate.*

Do you say as you do and do as you say? Think about how people act on a day-to-day basis. In hybrid workplaces, you may need to be intentional about it, but caring can come across in little ways. Rituals can have huge impact. Start with saying hello to everyone you pass when you get to the office. Send a short email every Friday thanking your team for something they did. Bring in breakfast every Monday. Use ten minutes at the beginning of staff meetings as an opportunity for everyone to share something or someone they are grateful for. Be creative. Make it small so it will be easy to do. And keep it as a recurring event. Perhaps ask everyone to add a recurring event to his or her calendar: Do a random act of kindness today. At the next staff meeting, give time for everyone to share what he or she did. The goodwill and positive energy will multiply.

TWO CULTURES

Hybrid workplaces are prime breeding grounds to create two cultures. And that is not a good thing. Separate remote and office cultures will be created unless managers and teams make a concerted effort to connect the team wherever and whenever they work. Without integration there can be schisms in teams, a breakdown in communication, bad will, and decreased productivity. Without connections that include everyone, remote culture may yield a *Zoom ceiling* for some workers. Coined by industrial-organizational psychologist Elora Voyles, a Zoom ceiling is the glass ceiling for remote workers. This barrier will affect remote workers as they may be passed over for promotion in favor of in-office coworkers.[9] This can unfairly impact women and minorities, who tend to prefer work from home flexibly.

Ensuring your team has one culture entails bridging remote and office workers, ensuring team-wide communication and collaboration standards, holding one-on-one meetings, establishing rituals to build interpersonal glue, and using fair evaluation methodologies.

This chapter described components of culture that you can impact. The following chapters explain how to build a culture to be proud of and become an inspirational leader—one that will nourish individual employees, keep your team engaged and contribute to your organization's success.

Chapter Seven

Change

In section I, different options and guidelines were presented to help you decide what model of the workplace might be right for your organization. Once a desired change has been decided on, your organization and leaders need to appreciate that for this change to take place, each individual will change his or her feelings, attitudes, and behaviors. Change happens when each person is brought along the "journey of change." This personal transition process has been described by author and change expert William Bridges in his Bridges transition model, which features three stages of change: ending, neutral zone, and new beginnings.[1] The steps may overlap with each other. They give time, space, and attention to each individual's needs, psyche, pressures, attitudes, behaviors, and so on to make the new hybrid model work. We address each of these stages in the following three sections.

ENDING: LET GO AND MODIFY

Where the organization wants to end up begins with where each individual is now. The actual transition to the end starts where you are. This sounds obvious, but change requires letting go of past assumptions, work processes, behaviors, belief systems, definitions of success, and even relationships. It is the time when you identify what you are losing and learn how to manage those losses. As a leader, consider what you need to let go of and remember to observe and check in as to what employees are thinking and feeling.

Transitioning your ideas, priorities, work processes, and so on requires you to reflect, modify, or let go of certain preconceived notions. These preconceived notions may include the following:

- **Believing it will be easy**

  In simple words, change is hard. You'll need to spend time and effort revising priorities, thinking, speaking, brainstorming, problem solving, and just being uncomfortable. **Action Step:** Acknowledge that change is often hard.

- **Functioning on automatic pilot**

  This is the one thing you *must* let go of. Leadership styles and behaviors become inherent in your daily lives. Most leaders don't consciously think about how they lead. Moving to a hybrid work environment requires questioning past behavior and becoming very conscious of every decision, value, and behavior you engage in. **Action Step:** Identify one thing that you feel comfortable doing and always do. Ask yourself, "How will that work, or not, in a hybrid world?"

- **Having the conviction that the only and best way to work is for everyone to be in the office Monday through Friday, 9 to 5 (keeping in mind we haven't seen a 9 to 5 standard for decades)**

  If you have decided to move to a hybrid workplace, you also need to let go of the conviction that full-time in office is the only and best way to work. Everyone in the office on weekdays at standard times is one of the pillars of a full-time, in-office model. By definition, hybrid workplaces question and move to different models of where and when people work. **Action Step:** If you're not convinced that hybrid work is the way to go, try to figure out why you don't want to let go of that belief. Do not start to change your work environment until you're convinced that's the way to go. Speak with employees and get feedback about what matters to them, what they value about the current work model, and what they are looking for in a hybrid model.

- **Believing that people don't really work when they're not in the office**

Studies for years have indicated that productivity either increases or isn't impacted when working from home. For example, Microsoft found 82 percent of employees were more productive when working from home.[2] The National Institutes of Health also reported working from home yielded increased productivity.[3] And one study found a 13 percent increase in performance for home workers.[4] **Action Step:** Consider what it will take to assume good intentions. Consider shifting your attitude from "Trust needs to be earned" to "Mistrust needs to be earned," and be conscious of how your attitude will impact the rollout.

- **Suspecting that hybrid work is bad for morale**

The best way to determine the impact of hybrid work is simply to ask your staff. On the other hand, if you want to decrease morale, introduce heavy surveillance. A *Fast Company* article sums up the point: "Virtually looking over employees' shoulders isn't just bad for privacy. Research shows it could also be bad for business."[5] **Action Step:** If you are still convinced that people don't work when they're not in the office, ask them. They'll be able to tell you what they're working on.

- **Measuring employees by how much time they spend in the office**

Which would you rather have, employees in the office and looking busy or employees working from home and being busy? How people appear or where they work shouldn't matter. You can measure face time, or you can measure productivity. We recommend the latter. **Action Step:** Think about it. Is being busy the same as working? Rather than spending your time observing when employees come and go, define, and measure deliverables. In the end, meeting goals matters more than keeping seats warm.

- **Providing little structure**

Working without clear roles and responsibilities or standard processes is not good leadership even when everyone is in the office. If you've been leading with that lack of clarity, chances are your organization is small and you can get away with it. Other scenarios might be that you're not getting the highest level of performance from your employees, productivity is lower than it should be, or you have high turnover. Leadership requires clarity and guidelines. Little or no structure just doesn't work in a hybrid world. **Action Step:** Consider your personal leadership style. Do you like to give people a lot of leeway? If so, think about what it would take to push your comfort zone or what resources you could use to provide more organizational structure, including clarifying deliverables, roles, and responsibilities. Starting a hybrid model is an opportunity to provide structure where there hasn't been any in the past. Whether or not employees like what is being offered, they will appreciate clarity and consistency.

- **Communicating only one way**

Whether your default communication style is email, phone, IM, video, or meetings, with people working in different locations and at different times you'll need to add to your repertoire. Communication is one of the 7 Cs of leadership. **Action Step:** Identify how you prefer to communicate: where, when, with whom, and for what does it work best? Consider where it is breaking down. Is your inbox full of unread emails? How long does it take for you to respond to an IM? Are you in back-to-back meetings? Or worse, double or triple booked? Does your team need help with this too? Be thoughtful about how you will announce the new hybrid model. Plan on rolling out in multiple ways, including written communications, live town halls, video team meetings, individual meetings, a formal marketing campaign, and so on.

- **Connecting via drop-bys**

Connecting with your team is essential, and drop-bys are an excellent way to connect. However, in a hybrid world serendipitous drop-bys aren't always available. You'll need to add new ways to connect with your team. We appreciate that connecting takes time. But it should be at the top of your priority list. Again, connection is one of the 7 Cs. **Action Step:** Consider the way you connect with individuals and how your team connects. Is it scheduled or random? What would it take for you to connect differently? Pick up the phone? Send a personal email? Spend part of a meeting off topic? During the rollout, connecting with your team should be planned and consistent. Ideally this is done while everyone is in the office to minimize misunderstandings. Once a message has been delivered, drop-bys can be used to check in. The challenge is to make sure you drop-by everyone's desk.

- **Accepting the self-sabotaging idea "I don't have time"**

Allot time for the tasks that reflect your priorities. President Dwight D. Eisenhower was well-known for the Eisenhower principle of time management: "I have two kinds of problems: the urgent and the important. The urgent are not important, and the important are never urgent."[6] His philosophy of time management means being effective as well as efficient. If you prioritize your work based on its level of importance and urgency and consider moving to a hybrid workplace important but not urgent, it will never happen. It is your choice whether you free up time by shifting priorities and moving things in or out of your important-urgent box of activities. **Action Step**: Consider what you will let go of, or do differently, to make time for the hard work of making a hybrid work. The rollout will take a lot of time. Plan for it and block out time for communicating the new hybrid model. **Action Step**: Do your homework. Reflect on the reasons you are considering this move. Speak with leaders inside and outside your organization. Listen to your employees. Consider engagement, retention, desired culture, priorities, profitability, and other core issues. When you are ready to let go of or alter beliefs, values, actions, and priorities and start incorporating new ones, you're ready to move to the next stage of change.

NEUTRAL ZONE: ROLL OUT THE HYBRID WORK MODEL

Once you've made progress toward the ending stage, you can move to the neutral zone. This is when the old work model isn't gone but the new model hasn't become the new norm. It is the space where patterns are changing and change is stressful. You can't be on autopilot—leaving the house five days a week at the same time, stopping at the same coffee shop, taking the same commute route, stopping by the same two coworkers on the way to your desk, and so on until the end of the day when you start your commute home. There are different neuropathways for learned behavior and new behavior. The neutral zone is living between the old autopilot and the new autopilot. Psychological, behavioral, and cognitive processes are changing. This is the core of the transition process.

People's responses to the rollout of the new hybrid model will vary. Organizations need to appreciate that every individual changes at a different pace. Some people welcome change, other people find it hard to change. This is independent of whether they want hybrid work. Regardless of how the new policy is announced, companies should have leadership below the enterprise leader prepared and available for questions and discussions about what the implications for an employee's individual circumstances are. Once the enterprise has decided on a new hybrid model, it is up to each leader and team to make it work. Each leader will deal with the policy differently. This in turn will impact the specifics and journey each person will go through.

For example, one of our clients with a three to four days per week in-office requirement had two leaders who dealt with the policy in different ways. They both had highly skilled employees who did not want to come into the office every day but accepted that they would have to come in at least three days every week. There was a buzz around the company. Each team was wondering what their boss would decide. Everyone put his or her life on hold until his or her respective leader decided how to deal with the policy. Some people held off on moving. Others struggled with committing to daycare options. And others were just upset because they didn't want to change the activities that they were able to do while working at home. Could they continue the mid-afternoon cycling class? How many new clothes would they need to buy? Would this impact their sleep patterns? The unknown was stressful for everyone.

Michelle was a leader who'd made a swift decision that left no room for interpretation or flexibility. Michelle thought that was fair. She dealt with the change, made a decision, and wanted to move on. She said it was important to have team meetings on a weekly basis, felt it was best for morale, and wanted everyone in the office from Monday to Thursday. Starting the following Monday, Michelle didn't feel there was anything to discuss. The decision had been made. For some people, although they didn't like the answer, they could make this dramatic change at once. Most of the team wasn't going along so easily, however; they said it was a lot to adjust to and wanted time to ease into the change. But mostly they wanted an opportunity to discuss it. Although they did show up for work that Monday, they spent a lot of time complaining to each other. Here's the paradox: Had Michelle invested more time by engaging her team in addressing the complexities and challenges of the change, she would have lost less time when the new policy took hold. She ended up with a distracted team. She didn't give them time to work through the transition—either emotionally or logistically. One month later, three team members quit.

Jean was a leader who made a different choice. She polled her employees when the policy was announced. Jean found six employees with personal issues impacting their ability to come into the office four days per week. While she preferred everyone in the office four days per week, she faced losing six valued employees who would be hard to replace. Jean therefore announced a three-month trial: Monday to Wednesday would be office days. She explained that teamwork and meetings were to be scheduled on those days. In two months, they would re-evaluate the plan. She recognized that people needed time to adapt. Two months later, productivity and morale were fine. And no one had quit. Three months later, everyone agreed to work three and one-half days per week in the office.

Action Step: Acknowledge that each team member will be going through his or her own transition both psychologically and logistically.

Action Step: Take time to listen. Giving your team space to talk and process the transition is a gift.

Action Step: Breathe. It's going to take time.

NEW BEGINNINGS:
TAKE ONE SMALL STEP AT A TIME

We appreciate that the process will require a lot of time, many emails and meetings, more emails and meetings, writing, re-writing, and so on. As you can see from Michelle's approach and Jean's approach, making changes one step at a time will allow your employees to adjust to and evaluate what works. Moreover, they will stay engaged. Each individual will learn the nuances of making a hybrid policy work, but they will need your help and patience.

You will be faced with bringing out the best in each team member and maintaining consistency while maximizing productivity. We recommend you choose one thing to try at a time. Re-read the 7 *C*s, highlight those that are relevant to you, then pick the easiest one to start with. Yes, start with the easiest one. Small things will get noticed.

If you haven't already, here's one small thing to do: Ask each of your employees how he or she is doing, and when someone says, "Fine," ask again.

We've said it before: Change is hard. As with any change, there will be breakdown points when you're implementing the new policy. Be on the lookout for these. If any occur, you'll need to change something. Again.

Leaders should be wary of:

- moving toward micromanagement due to lack of trust
- overcompensating by adding unnecessary meetings
- lacking intentionality in connecting and inspiring teams
- undermining the time needed to lead the team and time needed to do the work by shifting priorities
- treating some employees differently than others
- not following company guidelines
- not clarifying roles and responsibilities
- not partnering with your team to develop a team charter and communication guidelines
- failing to notice when morale is down and your team is feeling disconnected from one another

Employees should be wary of:

- insufficiently communicating with supervisors about what they're working on
- working at home on random days without informing teammates
- stopping work early without informing their boss
- not being reachable on a work-from-home day
- not putting in effort to connect with the team when they're in the office
- zooming consistently with the camera off
- allowing themselves to be distracted by multitasking
- covering up for another employee and leaving the boss in the dark

• failing to meet requirements for deliverables

Change isn't just hard, it's also a process, and each employee will go through their own personal journey of how and when their thoughts, feelings, and behaviors adapt to the new hybrid work model.

The best time to start is now. Pick one thing from this chapter that will stick with you before moving to the next chapter. Take one small step at a time.

Chapter Eight

Connection

You are busy. Your job may take up most of your time, so you don't have time to build connections—or as Julie calls it, *interpersonal glue.* But for you as a leader, building interpersonal glue with your team *is* your job. A connected team with lots of interpersonal glue is productive and engaged with high morale and low turnover. Unlike teams with little or no glue, connected teams use interpersonal glue to work through challenges and conflicts.

One of Julie's clients was chief technology officer at a global consumer products company. He was pleasant, well-known for his technical expertise, and very busy, and he didn't feel he had time for nonwork conversations. While he was liked, he had minimal interpersonal glue with his team, morale was low, and the team splintered at times of conflict. He then decided to allow space for his team to cultivate interpersonal glue. At one meeting, he allowed fifteen minutes to be spent with jovial sparing about basketball teams and March Madness bracket predictions. To his surprise, the fifteen minutes created bonds and goodwill that allowed the team to resolve other contentious issues. In all likelihood, had his team spent all sixty minutes discussing these issues and nothing else, sans interpersonal glue, the meeting would have ended where it started: with problems to be solved.

Making connections is as essential as meeting deliverables. While the people on your team may meet deliverables, over time if "I don't know you" or "I don't like you" prevails among them, they won't continue to be as effective as if they'd made connections. Productivity will go down.

Such was the case in 2020. As the pandemic required us to work at home, organizations marveled at the high rate of productivity that continued throughout the year. During the same year, we observed high rates of anxiety, depression, and burnout. In one study with SAP and Qualtrics, over 40 percent of employees experienced a decline in mental health during this time.[1] In fact by the end of the year, Julie found the most prevalent complaint from clients was, "I'm exhausted," and they would go on to describe the stress of working alone and on teams that were out of touch—literally and figuratively. Work connections consisted of looking at two-inch squares of people's faces on computer screens for meetings, all centered around the work itself. Interpersonal connections were just not on the agenda.

Before 2020, connections and engagement occurred frequently, randomly, and spontaneously. You might be entering an office building, walking by someone's desk, bumping into someone in the office kitchen, grabbing lunch, or meeting in a conference room. They were a natural part of the workday and didn't require extra thought. The random interactions occurred seemingly without effort. But building personal connections and interpersonal glue requires effort. Relationships are essential and need sustenance.

Not taking care of relationships is costly. According to a large Cigna study, loneliness could cost the US economy over $406 billion a year.[2] Of note, while the report was published in March 2020, when employees started working from home due to the pandemic, the data was collected before 2020. In addition, Cigna found that 61 percent surveyed felt lonely in large part due to lack of social support. Another study conducted by BetterUp[3] found that high levels of belonging were related to a decrease in turnover and sick days and an increase in job performance and employer net promoter score, resulting in an annual savings of $52 million for a 10,000-person company.

Julie's research on social support on and off the job found that the best predictor of general well-being was social support at work. More than friends and family, it is our coworkers who impact our overall satisfaction and productivity. Since those findings, Julie has consistently said to clients, "Be nice to your coworkers." This is a tall task for some more than others.

In hybrid work environments, we can't count on bumping into someone in the office, so we need to be intentional in building relationships. This is essential for maximizing productivity, engagement, mental health, and happiness. Everyone should be reminded to cultivate interpersonal glue by being intentional about where, when, and how to connect.

Leaders need to facilitate connections with their teams. Two parallel tracks are operating: the work track and the personal track. Bosses who only focus on getting the work done generally have teams with poor morale, limited engagement, higher absenteeism, and the like. Leaders who build interpersonal glue have happier, more engaged, and more productive employees.

Try one or more of these action steps. The more the better.

BUILD YOUR OWN INTERPERSONAL GLUE WITH YOUR DIRECT REPORTS AND THE TEAM AT LARGE

1. Create rituals at the beginning and the end of the day

- In a hybrid world where everyone can be connected all the time, it is important to help employees establish rituals to maintain boundaries between work and homelife. A daily hello and goodbye will both build connections and create healthy boundaries.
- Every morning—yes, every day—be intentional about saying good morning to everyone. If you are in the office, pass everyone's desk—even if you have to walk out of your way—and say good morning. For the virtual folks, send an IM, Slack, or email in which the subject line is Hello with ideally a short message or reminder of something timely. Greet people when you arrive in the office or sign-on in the morning.

2. Do virtual or live walk-arounds

- In addition to, or instead of, morning and afternoon greetings, commit to fifteen to sixty minutes per day to walk the floor or call members of your team and ask how they're doing. For people who are working out of the office, a check-in call reminds them that you're thinking of them and creates a bond. And if the call goes to voice mail, leave a short message.

3. Regularly schedule check-ins

- Ideally, these will be at least weekly and in person. If that's not possible, schedule a call or video meeting. Check-ins can be part of one-on-one meetings or a separate meeting. The point is to see how each person is doing. Start with "How are you?" and if the response is a typical "Fine," ask additional questions.
  When employees feel listened to, they will feel cared for and connected.
- Check-ins should be predictable and something others can count on. Don't cancel check-ins. When you do, the message to your direct report is, "You're not a priority of mine." If you can't make your regularly scheduled time, reschedule within a week.

4. Add additional check-ins as needed

- When something is going on that is out of the ordinary, increase the frequency of your check-ins. When your employees face challenges, the best thing you can do is let them know you care, will listen, and will provide support. Ideally these will be in-person meetings, perhaps for breakfast, coffee, or lunch. And if those aren't possible, call, text, email, IM, Zoom—anything to make sure you reach out to the person. Following are some examples of employee challenges. When things like this happen, this isn't the time to cut them out. This is the time to increase, as necessary.

  o Work suddenly gets very busy.
  o The employee has something unusual going on whether it be work related, personal, or health related.
  o You notice any change in the employee's behavior.

5. Schedule regular office hours

- Office hours are the hybrid equivalent of an open-door policy. In the office, if your door is open and you're in your office, an employee can determine if you're available by popping his or her head in and asking. In a hybrid world, shared calendars can let employees know if you're in the office, but they won't know if you're able to chat. And since "Zoom bombing" isn't a good way to ask something, scheduling regular office hours will let your team know when they can virtually or literally stop by. Let your team know when these times are and let them know the best way to contact you. Call? Open a Zoom link? Text? If you commit to a few hours per week and leave them unscheduled, your team will feel your support and connection even if they never stop by. And if no one shows up for office hours, you have time to catch up on emails, work on a new team strategy, or organize your desk.

6. Grab a meal, coffee, or take a walk

• There is nothing better than connecting with someone outside the office. Take some time out of the day to get to know someone better, provide support, chit-chat, express appreciation, and so on. The only caveat is whatever you do for one, you must do for all.

BUILDING INTERPERSONAL GLUE
AMONG THE TEAM AT LARGE

1. Let's have lunch

• In a hybrid world you cannot count on the randomness of bumping into someone or joining people you see leaving the office. Hence, create a lunch schedule and publish it. It could be

  ◦ pairings within the team—people who don't know each other; people who don't work together; a new employee with a long-time team member, and so on
  ◦ small groups: random within a team, across departments, intact groups
  ◦ you and one of your team members (just make sure you eventually meet with everyone)

When rolling out the program, be very specific about who is responsible for sending the first email, who is responsible for picking the place where they're meeting, and so on. Ideally these lunches can be when all participants are scheduled to be in the office. But if that's not possible, people can still lunch together virtually.

And if possible, pay for lunch.

2. Build in pre-meetings

- Once again, what happens without planning in face-to-face meetings is that the first one to fifteen minutes is spent shooting the breeze. This happens naturally as attendees slowly arrive. Employees rarely apologize for being a few minutes late for an in-person meeting.
- In contrast, if you're late for a virtual meeting (one minute late, you apologize; three minutes late, you profusely apologize), everyone has to wait for you to get to work.
- Inspirational leaders realize that shooting the breeze is crucial work too. That's why you should build a pre-meeting into every meeting whether the meeting's in-person, virtual, or hybrid. Be intentional and set guidelines for your team so that whether or not you are at any given meeting, your team knows they should take time at the beginning to find out how the pizza is at the new pizza place that opened.

3. Use ice breakers

- A type of pre-meeting that is good for a laugh and builds interpersonal glue is an ice breaker. These are quick and easy ways for people to get to know one another. They don't require any preparation. Simply throw out a prompt, and everyone shares. We recommend you make it a ritual at the beginning of one recurring meeting, and you can rotate who is responsible for generating the prompt or have the owner of the meeting do so. Here are some possible prompts:

  - What do you see outside your window?
  - What's in the room next to you?
  - Share a fun fact or show everyone an item of interest.
  - What were the last three things you purchased online?
  - What's your favorite TV show?
  - Do a short breathing or visualization exercise.
  - Play some music at the beginning of the meeting as people are arriving.

4. Provide shout-Outs

- Everyone wants praise, acknowledgment, and appreciation. One of the best ways to increase morale and interpersonal glue is to provide regular shout-outs. Pick a frequency that works for you, but we recommend once per week. We've never met anyone who complained that they got too much of it. Here are some pointers to keep in mind:

- As the leader, be intentional about praising someone or something that has been done. Acknowledge someone's efforts or thank them for doing something, making sure you rotate who you are doing it for and in time offer praise to everyone.
- Pick one person every week and ask everyone to share something that person has done to be helpful or see that a job was well done.
- Pick one person every week to say something positive about each member of the team.
- Remember to make these authentic. These don't take a lot of time. Just be intentional and remember to do them.

5. Help your team generate team rituals

- A ritual is something that takes place on a regular basis. Repetition breeds familiarity and comfort, and it decreases stress. Consider how it feels when you arrive at your coffee shop in the morning and the barista has your coffee waiting for you. Aside from getting your caffeine fix, the familiarity reduces stress. For contrast, think how you'd feel showing up at your coffee shop to see an Out of Business sign. Help your team generate team rituals but remember that it's important that they develop it themselves. Here are some examples of team rituals. Keep in mind they should not require a lot of effort unless your team wants them to.

  - On an in-office day, rotate who brings in bagels or some treat. Food helps bring people together. Reimburse team members if possible.
  - Schedule meetings that you begin with everyone sharing a moment of pride they experienced. Team members can also try "joy spotting" (noticing something joyful) or even proposing a challenge of the week.

- ○ Identify a day when everyone is encouraged to do a random act of kindness before work and then share what they've done with the team.
- ○ Give time or money to a charity as a team.

6. Encourage networking

- In a hybrid world, not only do you lose serendipity when working with your team, your integration and connections with other groups is limited. Your team should have a cadence and have a predictable schedule. However, depending on your organization's policy, it is likely that other departments have different cadences and different in-office schedules.
- Several of Julie's clients have policies that include different scheduling options for different parts of the organization. Some have client-facing versus office-support with different schedules. Others vary their schedules based on team size. And others vary schedules based on whether they are an individual contributor or part of a team where their work is more interdependent.
- Intentionality is necessary. Networking events can be an excellent forum for people to build organic connections with people from different areas. Here are some event examples:

  - ○ Informal, relatively large events that bring people from different areas together. Happy hours or breakfasts are options. But the limitation of these is they are outside normal work hours and may be hard for some to attend.
  - ○ Themed gatherings or lunch-and-learns that include time for informal chatting.
  - ○ In-office show and tell. Rotate among teams or departments and have everyone share the nuances of what they do. Julie has found that teams often don't know what other teams do and even less what other departments do.

7. Create special-interest groups

- Create a space or process so that on-going groups can be created. Once the group is created, the group itself can be self-led and determine its own mission, structure, frequency of meeting, and so on. Here are some suggestions:

- Have one department solicit feedback about interest groups that employees gravitate toward. Based on these results, that department can create affinity groups and open up membership to the entire organization.
- Create a platform where employees can organically form groups, like a meet-up.
- Create cross-function groups that employees can join and then decide on an agenda, a purpose, and so on.

8. Create a mentorship program

- A mentorship program should be something that both mentors and mentees can get something from. Here are some pointers for developing a program:

  - Assign a department to develop and run the program. Provide resources for them to create the program, solicit participation, and provide training for mentors and mentees on how to be an effective mentor or mentee. Julie has seen mentorship programs fail because the participants were not given enough structure or training.
  - Solicit members within your organization to become a volunteer committee to organize and run the program. Provide resources to help them launch and run the program.
  - Provide company-wide training on how to be a mentor and ask participants to mentor junior members of the organization. This fulfills the need to be intentional about providing informal, but necessary, on-the-job training for junior-level employees.

9. Conduct team-building activities—off-site and on-site.

- Off-sites are times to bring your team together for team building. They can take place out of the office at a restaurant, hotel, conference center, spa, and so on; or they may be on-site, which in the case of a hybrid world may be special enough to have everyone in the office. Here are some things to keep in mind:

○ Off-sites should always include time to build interpersonal glue. While fun is important, having opportunities to get to know each other better will be invaluable in driving team engagement, connections, and ultimately productivity.

○ The agenda may also focus on specific work such as strategic planning, addressing changes, and tackling big projects or clients.

○ When going through a re-organization or departmental and team changes (new team members, for example), off-sites are good for clarifying roles and responsibilities, generating work processes, or solving work problems.

○ When there is team discord or morale is low, off-sites can address the discord, provide a forum to repair strained relationships, create an atmosphere of good intentions, and build interpersonal glue.

○ Depending on the agenda, you may be able to facilitate or perhaps leverage the skills and support of your HR department or even hire external consultants.

Whenever Julie has facilitated off-sites, regardless of the agenda, the feedback is consistent: Meeting with coworkers was the most valuable part of the off-site.

Chapter Nine

Communication

Intentionality. We have spoken about it from the beginning. We have spoken about it throughout the book. We would suggest to you that getting off automatic pilot regarding how you communicate is one of the biggest sticking points in hybrid work.

Leaders are responsible for considering what employees need to hear and then communicating that information. Clear and consistent communication is not only the responsibility of every leader; it is also essential in building trust in that leader and within the entire organization. Has anyone ever said to you, "Do as I say and not as I do"? While leaders probably won't say that exact expression, they may act inconsistently from what they say. Rather, our mantra for you is, "Say as you do, do as you say."

Your team could not read your mind when you were all in the office full-time. They certainly cannot read your mind when they are working in the office sometimes and working remotely other times.

Consider John, a department head for a large consumer product company. His message to the team as to the way to communicate with him was, "Stop by my office. I hate emails and don't read them." While that wasn't good collaborative leadership back in the day when we lived in an office-only work world, it definitely won't work in a hybrid world. Chances are at any given time some of his teams will be working remotely. Just like John, most people have a communication modality of choice. Or maybe it is just a habit that has not been questioned for years. When you're faced with a hybrid work environment, how you commu-

nicate becomes even more important. Different schedules, work locations, preferences, and cultures all yield a mishmash of communication
that if it were clarified and cleaned up, you'd have extra time to read
that book you have been putting off, getting to the gym (which you also
have been putting off), or maybe just leaving work at a reasonable hour.

Sarah, a senior executive at an advertising firm, was not a great
communicator but for reasons different from John's. Known to get
new clients, she would start working on projects and not tell the team
anything beyond the next day deliverable. She did not take the time to
communicate her strategy for the project, specify the deliverables, or
clarify the roles and responsibilities of team members. When everyone
was in the office full-time, the team learned to adapt. They regularly
asked for updates. Alternatively, some just quit because they didn't like
working in an environment where they were never given the big picture
and were only told what to do on an as-needed basis.

Sarah was vehemently against hybrid work. However, the organization went to a three-day per week in-office work schedule.
She needed to adapt. When we worked together, we coached Sarah
to have kick-off meetings for each engagement. She said what she
was going to do and did what she said. During these face-to-face
meetings, she shared the strategy, deliverables, and roles and responsibilities for everyone. She then followed up and continued to check
in with the team and include them in everything she did. Morale and
productivity increased. Turnover decreased.

Sarah moved from communicating on an ad hoc, need-to-know basis
to healthy communication. Communication in a hybrid world needs to
be planned—not in a formal way, but with forethought and regularity.

If you're having trouble planning what to say, think about what your
team needs to hear. Some common things that teams want to hear include the following:

strategy
changes
roles and responsibilities
deliverables
challenges
information
praise, acknowledgment, and appreciation

The three biggies are praise, acknowledgment, and appreciation. They are the most under-utilized and cost-effective way to demonstrate compassion, caring, value, and commitment and to build morale, engagement, motivation, productivity, goodwill; the list goes on and on.

Praise: That is giving someone a compliment like "Good job." Do not literally say that, though. It comes across as an insincere platitude. Instead, taking the time to say something specific is a valuable and cost-effective way to demonstrate compassion. Tell them, "Great job on figuring out that complex analysis" or "It is quite impressive how you handled that difficult client." One of Julie's clients once told her, "I can even remember what I was wearing the last time I received praise. It was five years ago. Finally, I just quit. I should have quit six years ago."

Acknowledgment: This is observing good behavior and telling the person what you observed. This is also a good way to teach someone something by confirming that he or she did something right. The individual will get confirmation that his or her good decision resulted in a positive outcome. Hence, the person knows what to continue to do. He or she will also feel good about getting noticed. This is yet another cost-effective and under-utilized way to motivate, engage, and increase productivity for team members. Tell someone something like, "I've seen you speaking up more in meetings" or "Your calm voice in yesterday's meeting was helpful in decreasing tension" or "Your slides in yesterday's presentation were well-organized and the graphics aligned with the client's brand."

Appreciation: This is simply saying "Thank you." Follow it with a specific reason for the gratitude: "I appreciate the way you . . ." Employees who feel appreciated will go the extra mile and feel valued. A common driver for employees feeling disengaged is feeling they are giving and producing but their work and hence they themselves are not appreciated. If someone has been working long hours on a project, simply say, "I appreciate you've been putting in extra hours." Or perhaps say something like, "Thank you for being patient in dealing with this difficult client."

Be mindful to include all members of your team based on what they do regardless of factors such as where they work or who they are.

WHAT'S GETTING THROUGH?

If we're going to discuss strategies for collaboration, including utilizing the different communication modalities that we have, we first need to explore what is getting through from speaker to listener.

Remember when you were a kid and played the game telephone? For those of you who never played it, the game of telephone started with one person whispering a statement into another person's ear. The second person then had to repeat the statement to a third person. The third person then had to repeat the statement to a fourth person and so it continued until the last person, at which point the last person said aloud what he or she had heard. Inevitably there was a discrepancy between what had been whispered by person one to person two and what was said out loud by the last person. So what started as "Juan Garcia went fishing in a boat on White Lake and caught four fish that we ate for dinner" might end up something like "John Jones was sitting in a boat and baked four fish." Not that any of us thought of this when we were eight years old, but there were in fact five factors that impacted what was heard and what got communicated.

These are the five factors that impact communication:

Who you are—This includes your background, education, personality, values, occupation, mood, ethnicity, first language, enjoyment of sports or games; the list goes on and on.

Your relationship with the speaker or the audience—Do you know the person or members of the group well? Do you like them? Are they the same background or ethnicity? Do they like you?

Nonverbal: vocal qualities—The volume, speed, clarity, and tone of the speaker's voice. Can you understand the speaker? Is he or she talking loud enough for you to hear? Is the speaker speaking too loud? Does he or she think this is funny? Does the speaker seem happy or aggravated?

Nonverbal: body language—The speaker's facial expressions, posture, movement, gestures. Is he or she smiling? Is he or she animated? Does the speaker put separation between you and him or her by sitting on the other side of a table or crossing the arms? What physical surroundings has the speaker created?

Verbal: content—And finally, the actual words being communicated.

Understanding yourself, how you come across, and how you take in information is where we begin, but it's the relationships you have with others that matter—the interpersonal glue between you and them. It becomes very important when dealing with challenging situations, conflict, or just negative emotions. These are a few of the circumstances that enhance the impact of voice qualities and body language on whether words are heard.

Numerous people have theorized about the different components of communication and what gets through. Experts generally concur that between 70 and 93 percent of our communication is nonverbal—that is, most of our communication derives from vocal characteristics and body language. Psychologist Albert Mehrabian's 1960s research, documented in his book *Silent Messages*, was a pioneer study in nonverbal communication, and his work may be particularly pertinent to challenging workplace situations, because he focused on the communication of emotions. In one of his studies, participants had to rate the feelings of a speaker after listening to him or her say different words. The words spoken and the speaker's tone of voice sometimes didn't match, and when they didn't, the tone of voice determined what emotion the listeners heard. It's the same thing with movement. You won't be believed if you purse your lips, cross your arms, and then say, "I'm sorry I interrupted your presentation." Consider these current modes of communication and what they use to get their message across:

- face-to-face, in-person meetings—facial expressions, full body language, vocal tone, and words
- face-to-face, video meetings—facial expressions, upper body language, vocal tone, and words
- telephone or conference calls—vocal tone and words
- email/IM/Google docs/Slack—words

For decades researchers have explored the different components of communication. For example, psychologist Michael Kraus found that voice-only communication elicited the highest rate of accuracy.[1] That is, the ability to gauge our emotions, thoughts, and feelings about what is said is the most accurate when we're talking to each other. Kraus believed that we're better listeners when we tune some of the nonverbals out.

Since 2017, as video conferencing has become the norm, many people have weighed in on how effective video conferencing is for communicating and collaborating. In 2020 the BBC reported that excessive video conferencing has its costs, not the least of which is decreased energy and exhaustion.[2] Since 2020, the use of video conferencing has substantially increased.

As noted, the first thing that impacts communication is *you.* And if we consider your own change process, that affects how you communicate.

We all have different backgrounds, experiences, preferences, learning styles, jobs, and more, hence we have our own preferred communication style and modality. A hybrid work world necessitates reflecting on your default style and considering whether or not it's the most effective way to communicate. Most work is complex and requires different interactions with different people about different kinds of work. When it comes to communicating, one size doesn't fit all.

Julie has a user-friendly model that her clients find helpful in examining, evaluating, and modifying which communication modality will be best for each person and situation.

Begin with your current preferences. Do you prefer mostly emails? Phone calls? Video meetings? Face-to-face, scheduled meetings? Stopping by someone's desk? We're not suggesting you need to change everything. We are suggesting you be intentional about the communication modality you use.

Consider *how* you connect, and then for each modality, consider *who*, *what*, *where*, *when*, and *why*. Reflecting on each will give you confirmation, or guidance, on what technique to use.

The How

Synchronous (at the same time):

- face to face and live: scheduled or unscheduled meetings, casual drop-bys, going out for coffee, and serendipity, aka "water cooler conversations"
- video chat or conference: scheduled meetings
- phone call: scheduled meetings, ad-hoc unplanned calls
- collaborative tools: whiteboards, screen sharing

Asynchronous (at different times):

- email
- IM: one-on-one
- text-based: for example, Slack
- shared folders: for example, Google docs
- collaborative tools: for example, project management software

Now let's consider the who, what, when, where, and why for each of the modalities.

The Who

Number of people: The smaller the number of people and the more positive the relationships are between them, the more options you have. Larger numbers result in something getting lost whether it be relationship connection, information shared, participation, or synergy.

Audience and relationships: The better you know each other and are clear about the purpose of meeting, the more options you have. Determine the extent to which your group has interpersonal glue. It matters whether it exists or if instead there is unfamiliarity or tension within the group. And ask yourself: *Do I feel the need to impress someone?*

Hierarchy: What are the reporting relationships of the participants? Does it have an impact on dynamics?

Internal participants: Do they know the purpose and structure of the meeting? Does it matter? (We think it does.)

External participants: Will consultants or clients be involved? Do they have an agenda that is similar to or unlike yours?

The What

In terms of content, the more neutral it is, the more options you have. The more negative the content, the more mindful you need to be of the modality.

Positive versus negative: Positive content can be delivered via any modality. Praise, acknowledgment, and appreciation can take place in multiple ways. On the other hand, how you connect on something with negative content takes a lot of forethought. Negative content delivery needs to be carefully planned with the goal of having the person feel heard and then hearing you. In general, the more negative something is, the more the modality needs to afford opportunity for emotions to come through and be addressed. Face-to-face connections can give information over and above the words. Misinterpretations can be addressed in the moment. On the other end of the communication spectrum, emails provide only words, which give room for a lot of misinterpretation. You don't want someone getting offended when no offense was meant.

Complex versus a single or simple issue: The more complex the content is, the more mindful you need to be when choosing the modality. With complex issues or multiple opinions, there must be equal room for contributions to be made. In addition, what is the best way to get someone to engage and hear what's going on? In general, discussions should happen synchronously. Discussions should not take place via email. Information sharing or progressing on identified goals in which individual work is required is best suited for asynchronous communication. Email chains are effective for conversations that go in a single direction.

Formal versus informal: The more formal the connection, the more mindful you need to be in planning the modality. Formal infers structured presentation or formal relationships, and hence you need to control the communication. Formal connections generally afford as much room for mistakes—hence the ability to correct them—as informal ones. If controlling the message regardless of how it is heard is of utmost importance, then asynchronous approaches can work. If you need to deliver a message but want to control how it's heard, then synchronous methods are recommended because you can correct misinterpretations right away. This is a value of the Q and A section of a discussion.

The Where

In office: Working in an office gives everyone the opportunity to use any of the communication modalities. As such, in the past when everyone was in the office, you didn't have to be intentional about which one you used (albeit equity and inclusion factors needed to be considered). However, in a hybrid environment, choosing the right modality is important. In-office work affords the best opportunity to build interpersonal glue via in-person, face-to-face communication. Take advantage of it. And yet why do people who sit next to each other communicate via email? (see chapter 10).

Hybrid: If everyone's not in the same location, intentionality and fore-thought are required. For this reason, we suggest hybrid schedules be planned and not completely left to individuals to change as needed. Considering all the other challenges involved, one option that allows for synchronous, formal, informal, planned, casual, complex, and simple communication is the phone. Asynchronous modalities work too, albeit with this reminder: Get off the automatic pilot of using only email. Rather, use it wisely and cautiously.

All remote: All remote does not allow live, in-person communication, which is why it's frequently not the best model. Video meetings, calls, Slack, shared documents, emails, and IMs don't build inter-personal glue like live, face-to-face connections. With an all-remote policy you'll need to put in a lot of effort to include synchronous connections to ensure effective and accurate communication.

The When

Just because you need or want something now doesn't mean it's when others can or want to do something. Consider your preferences and reflect on whether they align with your employees' personal and work needs. Leaders are supposed to define deliverables, delivery dates, and priorities. Good leaders engage and empower their team in deciding when the work will get done to meet these deliverables.

Time sensitive: Time factors should be considered in advance. With advance planning, you can be thoughtful and intentional in deciding the best modality. It's when things aren't planned that there are fewer options and response time becomes the issue.

Response time: If you haven't planned, then response time becomes an issue. In addition, unexpected things arise.

The Why

Decision making: When the decision to be made involves limited choices—the difference between simple versus complex—and the decision-making process is clear, including who can decide what, the more options you have on how the decision is made.

Creative processes and brainstorming: When participants need to play off each other to yield the best results, both asynchronous and synchronous modalities can be complementary communication modalities. If the creative process or brainstorming will be richer with each participant generating ideas on his or her own, then individual, asynchronous contributions can be valuable steps before synchronous conversations.

Conflict resolution: Connecting to resolve a conflict requires planning. Face-to-face communication is ideal because emotions can be monitored, and this can be helpful in addressing the real issue. However, many people are conflict averse, and an email or IM may be the safer way to proceed.

Alignment: The greater the differences that must be aligned, the more thoughtful you need to be in choosing your communication modality. If there is a great disparity between the people or positions to be aligned, synchronous communication will allow for addressing pushback or misunderstanding in the moment. Asynchronous modalities may fuel the discrepancy because your team members may read your communication differently and then stew about it.

Sharing information: Once again, consider whether the information to be shared will be received as positive, negative, complex, or simple. Do you want to control the message and not have a discussion? Consider whether it's more efficient to have everyone in the same room or on the same call versus everyone taking their time composing the information they want to share. The latter scenario will involve the time each person will need to take to read, review, or listen to that information.

Collaboration: If your communication is for the purpose of collaborating, well, that's a chapter unto itself—the next chapter. Collaboration is a word that Julie considers a big word. Big words are words that are vague and open to interpretation. One of Julie's favorite big words is *urgent*.

Collaboration is big and it's urgent.

Chapter Ten

Collaboration

As noted, *collaboration* is a big word, that is, a word with multiple meanings. It's overused and means different things to different people within an organization as well as different things between organizations.

One of Julie's clients is a large architecture firm in which collaboration is a firm value. They expect all members of the firm to be collaborative in the creative process and in any other team exercise. Given they design large, complex buildings, collaboration is mandatory to achieve cutting-edge work.

With *collaboration* being a big word at the firm, before the coronavirus pandemic when everyone was in the office full-time, most of the firm worked in ways that supported the spirit and practice of it. As such, the concept wasn't defined although it was easy to see in action. People gathered around tables, looking at documents and discussing. The energy of the open office plan allowed people to walk to each other's desk to converse. When someone was not being collaborative, their team would notice—in part because that behavior was relatively rare. Then teams and leaders could define what collaboration was not: not responding to emails; not putting work on ShareDrive; talking but not listening; missing meetings or only attending when something might be needed; writing abrupt emails; not including people on email chains who should have been included. Julie was called in to coach, on an individual basis, those leaders or their teams who were not working in collaborative ways.

When the firm necessarily moved to hybrid work, leadership experienced and heard about bad will and distrust developing because people weren't being collaborative. With a desire to maintain a positive culture with engaged employees, they reached out to Julie to discuss options to address the problem.

Modes of collaboration needed to be expanded, redefined, and standardized. The firm realized that without everyone in the office at same time, partners and the entire firm needed training on how to collaborate in a hybrid model. Julie worked with firm leadership on operational procedures and generating guidelines for new collaboration standards and behaviors. She then created a training model for the entire firm on new rules of engagement and collaboration and how to build connections, communicate, and collaborate in a hybrid world. After the training was delivered, feedback from employees was that stress, miscommunications, and working hours decreased while productivity and engagement increased. This highlighted the need to be intentional and set guidelines for communication and collaboration. And so we present you with factors to consider and guidelines to generate consistency in your organization.

In our hybrid world, Julie defines the big word *collaboration*: "Collaboration is connected communication."

Connect includes interpersonal glue.

Communicate includes giving and receiving.

The process encompasses the elements of communication identified in chapter 9.

Collaboration means connecting people.

1. You: What's going on for you? What do you want or need?
2. Your audience: What do they want or need?

Collaboration means communicating with one to five of these element.

1. Verbal: the words you use
2. Visual: the pictures, graphs, objects, drawings, and so on you use
3. Voice: how you sound
4. Body language: what your body is communicating
5. Appearance: how you look

Each collaboration modality has different characteristics. Reviewing the different characteristics of each modality, you can choose the *how* you work based on the *who, what, where, when,* and *why* you are working together. Different modalities and their elements impact the potential to build interpersonal glue (connect) and minimize miscommunication.

Table 10.1 identifies the range of building interpersonal glue and miscommunication potential for each modality.

Table 10.1

Modality	Element	Interpersonal Glue	Miscommunication Potential
Shared Documents	verbal, with visual	none	low
Online Whiteboards	visual, with verbal	none	low
Email	verbal, with visual	minimal	high
In-House IM Systems	verbal	minimal	high
Texts and Chats	verbal, with visual	moderate	high
Phone and Conference Calls	verbal and voice	high	low
Video Meetings	multiple elements	moderate to high	low
Live, Face-to-Face Meetings	multiple elements	high	low
Hybrid Meetings	multiple elements	moderate	moderate

Let's look at guidelines for the use and pitfalls of each modality.

SHARED DOCUMENTS

Shared documents are documents that are put on a shared drive that can be accessed by others, such as an Exchange, or documents that can be shared and easily modified by multiple people, such as Google Docs.

Shared documents are two-dimensional collaboration modalities that include verbal and visual dimensions such as words, pictures, graphics, and numbers. There is no emotion, no attitude, and there are no relationship factors. The opportunity for building interpersonal glue is nonexistent with shared documents. However, the opportunity for miscommunication is low as it is just the facts.

Opportunities for Use

- asynchronous work, but can also be used synchronously because employees can simultaneously create and edit documents
- sharing information efficiently when multiple people need it
- allowing iterative work that isn't synchronous
- allowing individual contributions to surface without groupthink
- documenting communications that need to be documented

Guidelines for Use

- Define the task and deliverable for each document.
- Standardize file labeling and where files should be located.
- Establish a process for multiple contributions, including decision makers.
- Track changes so participants know who made what contribution.
- Determine delivery dates.
- Ensure privacy settings to allow for controlled access of contributors.

Cautions

- Shared documents are a communication tool without any connection. Hence another modality must be used in concert with all shared documents. If you work on a document but don't let anyone know what you're working on, no one will know it's there.
- Since shared documents are individual work products, the work, including its degree of completion, is left to the individual contributor. The individual sharing the information may or may not be finished when the receiver needs it.
- When multiple people are simultaneously working on a document, individual contributions may clash or take the work in different directions.

ONLINE WHITEBOARDS

Online whiteboards can be used for the same purpose as a real whiteboard without the location limitation of a real whiteboard. The purpose of a whiteboard is to visualize thoughts, concepts, and ideas as well as to explain, teach, plan, and create.

Opportunities for Use

- similar to shared documents
- creative, iterative, non-linear thinking and brainstorming
- synchronous work, but can also be used for asynchronous contributions

Guidelines for Use

- Use as you would a shared document.
- Set contribution parameters to maximize input from everyone.
- Be clear about next steps when finishing a working session.

Cautions

- As whiteboards are generally used synchronously, be careful to avoid groupthink by encouraging diverse contributions.
- As the medium for conversation becomes visual, make sure everyone interprets the visuals correctly.

EMAIL

By far the most-used modality of collaboration, email, like shared documents, is a single dimension of communication sometimes with images or videos added. There is some opportunity for interpersonal glue or connection, but because there is no ability to use nonverbal dimensions of communication, the potential for miscommunication is high. (Although a pre-recorded video attached to an email can include nonverbal communication, it is still sent as a one-way communication.)

In contrast to shared documents, emails are sent *to* someone. Hence the first two elements to enter the collaboration equation are you, the receiver, and the other person, the sender. Once this personal component is added, your relationship with the person indirectly, and either unconsciously or consciously, enters the collaboration. We add emotions based on our mood and our relationship with the sender. But the intention of the writer, and the impact on the receiver, can be easily misaligned. Everyone can tell you what it feels like to receive an email written in all caps. It tells us the person is yelling. Well, maybe it does. Or maybe the person hit the Caps Lock button by mistake.

Julie was contacted by the EVP of the Consumer Marketing Department of a global media and entertainment company because the EVP was concerned about decreased productivity and morale. She felt that "people were not working well together." After interviewing the team and assessing how they worked together, Julie learned that although their hybrid model required them to be in the office at least three days per week, and their prime mode of communication was email. No one walked the halls. They sat at random desks so there were complaints that employees couldn't find each other. The kitchen was small. There was minimal shared space. There were complaints of withheld information, miscommunication, being taken off distribution lists, not being on the correct distribution lists, rude comments, poorly written emails, information sent to the wrong people, being on the To line as opposed to the Cc line, being on the Cc line instead of the To line, adding the boss to an email chain, people not responding in a timely manner, people not responding at all.

All these seemingly minor email mistakes were, in fact, not minor at all.

The mistakes were due to not taking the time to be thoughtful when composing emails, not considering the implications of where someone might be on a distribution list, not being respectful of each other's time, being passive-aggressive when adding someone's boss to a chain, decreasing work quality by not including the right people, missing deadlines because of lack of responsiveness—and on and on.

Upon hearing the feedback, the EVP wanted to hold an off-site to address the underlying issues that were being played out via acting out in emails and generate guidelines for engagement. The off-site began with Julie sharing the team feedback with everyone. Most team members were relieved to hear that they were not alone. The pervasive undercurrent of bad will was now front and center. Shifting the perspective to assume good intentions, the team was able to generate a list of guidelines to ensure open and consistent communication.

Julie helped the team on this journey by using the metaphor of having a birthday party for email communication and then generating department guidelines.

The To Line

If you're having a birthday party, the first thing you are mindful of is whom you invite. You do not randomly add people to your party list. Perhaps it's BFFs only. Or maybe the entire first-grade class. Do you want to invite the parents? Oops, no you don't want to invite the parents. That will ruin the fun and require extra cupcakes.

If you're a guest, don't bring a friend without asking and don't uninvite someone you had a fight with on the playground.

Translation to department guidelines: Include only people who need to *do* something on the To line.

Cautions: If you are not the owner of the email, do not add someone without confirming first with the email owner. Or if you are certain the owner will support your decision, state in the email why you are adding that person.

If you are not the owner of the distribution list, do not delete someone from the list without confirming with the owner, and the person affected, and then state in the email why you are removing the person.

The Cc Line

Move people to the Cc line who are not directly involved in doing something but need to know information in the email. For example, they just need to know what time to drop off and pick up their child.

Translation to department guidelines: The Cc line is only for people who need to know what's going on. Before adding anyone, ask yourself, Have they asked to be on the Cc list? If so, why? If not, why am I adding them? What do I expect them to do with the information?

The Bcc Line

I'm not sure anyone needs to be on the Bcc line. Maybe just your grandmother. She can't come but would love to know what's up.

Translation to department guidelines: Use the Bcc line sparingly and with caution.

When moving someone to Bcc once an email chain has started, tell everyone that you did it. For example, when you've introduced two people via email, one of the recipients may move you to the Bcc line to keep you informed but not involve you in the conversation.

The Subject Line

You could put something generic like "Come Celebrate" or worse, leave it blank. But if you write, "You're invited to Jamie's Birthday Party, January 10, 2030," your guests will be excited before they even read the email.

Translation to department guidelines: The subject line is the most important part of the email. Never leave it blank; make it as specific as possible.

Ideally, the subject line starts with what you expect the user to do with the email. For example, "Please respond by___"; "Decision Needed"; "Meeting Requested"; "Input Needed." Some teams agree on acronyms to include in emails. For example, *FYI* (For your information); *WFH* (Working from home); *PRB* (Please reply by); *NRN* (No reply necessary); *AR* (Action required); *EOD* (End of day); *TLTR* (Too long to read); *TL;DR* (Too long; Didn't read). After that, follow up with the specific request or issue. For example:

Approval Needed by 3/30/26: Team Off-site Budget
Meeting Request: Topic–Deliverables for Graystone Account
Decision Needed Re: New Intern Candidates

Long subject lines, with details, are encouraged. If appropriate, the entire content of the email can be in the subject line—for example, "Meet me in the cafeteria at noon" and "Colors for the masthead are green and blue." And if you add *EOM* (End of message) the reader will know there is nothing written in the body.

The Email Body

You could spend three paragraphs writing about all the options you considered for your birthday party, all the different food choices you considered, or why you chose Devin the Clown instead of Shawn the Juggler before you got to the location and time for your party. If so, some people may not get to the important facts. Or you could write a couple of lines describing how excited you are, the theme of the party, and when and where it is. If you do the latter, everyone will show up and you'll have a grand time. Or you could buy a card that has lines to be filled in.

Party: Christopher's 5th Birthday
Theme: Circus—Wear a costume
When: June 3, 2026, 2–4 p.m.
Where: 33 Main Street, New York, NY
RSVP: 211-212-3333

Translation to department guidelines: Less is more. Don't write long emails unless necessary. Also keep the following in mind:

Emails should be well-written with no spelling or grammatical errors.
Bullets and numbers help with clarity.
Emails should be sent during business hours.
Hostile emails should never be sent.

Given the pervasive use of email and the amount of time each of us spends writing and reading them, the personal problems that are exacerbated by miscommunication, the legal problems that ensue when emails are used improperly, and the mistakes, stress, and exhaustion they cause, there is an almost endless number of considerations when emailing.

Given it's a word-based collaboration tool and therefore there are no nonverbal dimensions, there is plenty of room for readers to interpret the words differently than the writer meant.

Think about your expectations and emotions after reading the subject line "Problems." If it's from your disrespectful boss, you are angry before you read it. If it's from your best friend whom you saw last night, you are worried. If it's from your mother who emails you with nonsense, you'll be annoyed. All these reactions hit you before you read the body. In short, the connection you have with the sender colors the words. These colors are the prime reasons for miscommunication. If you use them carefully and know your audience, emojis can help clarify spirit and intent.

Remember: Emails are a single-dimension collaboration modality with little room for interpersonal glue and a lot of room for misinterpretation. Emails that are neutral or positive in content can be written with ease. Emails that are negative in content must be written with thoughtfulness if at all.

Guidelines for Use

- Use emails to share information. They are not for complex discussions.
- Use Microsoft 'PowerPoint-ese'—that is, short statements, bullets, and numbers.
- Use Microsoft 'Word-ese' with care. If it's long, people won't read it anyway.
- Use the two-scroll rule: Anything you write should be able to be read with two thumb scrolls down a phone screen.
- Be mindful of whom you put on To, Cc, and Bcc lines.
- Write clear, detailed subjects.
- Review the standing distribution lists you own and delete unnecessary recipients.
- Ask to be removed from distribution lists that you don't need to be on.
- If the content is complex or negative, be very careful when drafting the email. Better yet, pick up the phone or schedule a meeting to discuss.
- Check your spelling and grammar.
- In general, expected response time on an email is within 24 hours except on non-business days.

Cautions

- Email's 24-hours-per-day availability leads to overwork, stress, and no boundaries.
- People don't read emails that are too long.
- Writing good emails takes time. As Mark Twain said, "I didn't have time to write a short letter, so I wrote a long one instead."
- Emails are legal documents.
- While one can rapidly respond back and forth, the response time is still receiver controlled. Hence senders may expect responses faster than receivers intend.
- Emails aren't good mechanisms for building interpersonal glue nor are they a substitute for meaningful, person-to-person communication.

- Group emails tend to become discussions. Discussions should be held in a meeting.
- Negative content or conflicts may be exacerbated by email.

IN-HOUSE IM SYSTEMS

At their core, in-house IM systems such as Slack are a single-dimension collaboration modality that includes verbal communication. However, like email, it is possible to add visual and audio attachments. In fact, in-house IM systems are very similar in use to email, and some companies prefer them to email. But in general, it's text communication.

As it is a words-only collaboration modality and it is messaging to someone, the opportunity for miscommunication is high. Relationship factors impact what gets heard.

One of Julie's clients was a med-tech company that added Slack to their communication platform to supplement email. However, the company founder complained that Slack was taking up too much time, including interrupting time she had set aside for strategic planning. Because Slack had been added as a tool to address immediate issues and simulate live discussions, she felt a need to not miss anything. However, channels started to multiply, and the problem became worse. She also felt scattered because she felt the need to be engaged constantly on emails and Slacks not to mention Twitter, Instagram, and their project management app. At the same time, the founder wanted to maintain culture, enhance collaboration, and decrease distractions. After reflecting on options and gaining input from her team, she removed several channels and set guidelines that included no Slack allowed between 8 to 10 a.m. and 5 to 7 p.m., no attachments on Slack, only email; and if you need to connect with anyone between 10 a.m. and 5 p.m., call them. Finally, and the biggest cultural shift, if you receive a call between 10 a.m. and 5 p.m. and you are not in a meeting, pick up the phone.

After one month, the feedback was consistent: People were less distracted, less stressed out, more productive, and getting to know their coworkers.

Opportunities for Use

*   short and simple communications
*   neutral context
*   a complex response not needed
*   a quick response needed

Guidelines for Use

*   Identify team guidelines for what to use IM for.
*   Define what the recommended response time is.

Cautions

*   Don't forget it's a legal document.
*   Keep in mind people read things in to words.
*   Don't overuse and expect an immediate response every time.
*   Shift to a call or meeting before a group chat gets complex or over-whelming.

TEXTS AND GROUP CHATS

Texts and chats can be private, one-on-one communications or group conversations. They may seem faster than email, but the speed of delivery is the same. And the speed of response rests with the receiver. You can ignore a text just as easily as you can ignore an email. Given that a nonaudio text is a single-dimension communication modality with some opportunity for interpersonal glue or connection, there is no ability to use a nonverbal dimension of communication, so the potential for miscommunication is high.

Julie was working with the department head of a large-scale commercial construction company who was complaining that his new boss had a reputation of being demanding, difficult, and a micromanager. In the middle of a meeting with Julie, he received a text from his new boss. After reading it, he got agitated. "See? He *is* demanding and a micromanager. He's yelling at me that I've got to work all weekend." Julie asked if she could read the message. It said, "The report is due at 4 on Monday." She read the text back to him in a calm, neutral tone and then asked, "Are you sure he's yelling? Seems like he's just telling you a fact. It says nothing about you working on the weekend." After pausing, the department head said, "Wow, maybe he's not a jerk after all."

Personal color or emotions can be added to texts via emojis and memes. They can be used to add context or emotions to clarify content. This can be valuable because content in texts tends to be more personal than in emails.

Once again, negative or critical content requires extra care and thoughtfulness.

Beware: Exclamation points are overused. Some people use three explanations points when they're happy or mad. If you feel an exclamation point's needed, only use one.

Opportunities for Use

- short and simple communications
- neutral context
- a complex response not needed
- a quick response needed

Guidelines for Use

- Define what the recommended response time is.

Cautions

- Don't forget texts can be obtained by outside sources.
- Remember that people read things into words.
- Don't overuse and expect an immediate response every time.
- Shift to a call or meeting before a group chat gets complex or overwhelming.

PHONE AND CONFERENCE CALLS

The phone has shifted from being an immediate way to connect with somebody to being used primarily for scheduled connections. Common practice is to schedule a conference call. In contrast, unscheduled phone calls generally are not answered. Rather, the receiver ignores the call, and the sender then leaves a voice mail. In this case, it is up to the receiver when to call back. This works fine when everyone is in the office full-time because you can stop by somebody's desk for a quick, unscheduled connection. However in a hybrid world, this has the potential to simulate stopping by somebody's desk.

As a two-dimension communication modality, the phone is verbal, voice communication. As a lot of emotion comes through the tonal qualities of one's voice, the potential to build interpersonal glue is high. And as the connection takes place live, the chance for miscommunication is low. This is because if there is a miscommunication, it is noticed immediately and can be corrected on the spot.

In a hybrid world filled with Zoom meeting after Zoom meeting, most people will breathe a sigh of relief when somebody requests a call instead of a video meeting.

Opportunities for Use

- a quick response needed to a simple question
- a scheduled meeting to discuss a complex or slightly challenging topic
- building interpersonal glue
- scheduling meetings rather than using an extensive email exchange to do the same thing
- collaborating on an urgent matter

Guidelines for Use

- If you're not committed to another person or work, answer every call.
- Be respectful of others' time.
- Keep unscheduled calls as short as possible.
- If you call and no one answers, either call back or leave a voice mail.

Cautions

- Don't use a phone call for negative or contentious discussions (although it's better than an email or text).
- Don't assume the person you are calling is available.
- Don't assume the person you are calling listens to voice mails.

VIDEO MEETINGS

Interactions over Zoom, MS Teams, Facetime, WebEx, and BlueJeans went from occasional use before the pandemic at many companies to regular use during the pandemic to mixed use in a hybrid world.

Video meetings are a multidimension communication modality of verbal and visual messaging that includes your voice, body language, and appearance. However, connecting over video is not the same as a face-to-face collaboration. In face-to-face collaborations, you look at one another. In video meetings, everyone looks at a camera. No person-to-person eye contact is possible. The content delivered may be the same, but technology can distort how it comes across. Your voice, body language, and appearance may be the same, but many things get lost when you're looking at a 2-inch-by-2-inch picture on your computer screen.

There is an opportunity to build interpersonal glue, but one must be intentional to do so.

In March 2020, when most companies moved their workforce to 100 percent remote work due to the coronavirus pandemic and people were in lockdown at home, Zooming was used to replicate in-office work. Although Zooming was initially viewed as a lifeline for collaboration, exhaustion set in after a few months, and it became clear that Zooming is not the same as in-person connecting.

Opportunities for Use

- people who want or need to meet but are not co-located
- people who want to share documents and simultaneously discuss

Guidelines for Use

- Ask yourself if you need to meet.
- Plan, plan, plan for the meeting.
- Include five to ten minutes of pre-meeting for building interpersonal glue.
- See to it that everyone is either on video or off video if possible.
- Keep it as short as possible.
- For meetings over sixty minutes, take a break.

- For meetings sixty minutes or shorter, allow a five-minute break for every twenty-five minutes of meeting time. Try the expression "fifty is the new sixty."

Now let's consider elements that impact collaboration and how they work within a video meeting.

Connections

If the participants have already met in-person and have a relationship, that relationship will continue to develop in the way it had already been established. If the participants are meeting for the first time, you need to be intentional about building interpersonal glue. Pre-meetings can build interpersonal glue through informal chat.

Communications

1. Verbal
   The words used during video and face-to-face meetings are similar.
2. Visual
   Smart galleries and virtual whiteboards allow people to contribute simultaneously.
   Easy-to-share documents supplement content and support simultaneous work.
3. Audio
   Vocal qualities during video and face-to-face meetings are similar.
   Emotions and tone are a bit harder to discern during a video meeting.
4. Body Language
   Person-to-person eye contact is not possible, and that limits the ability to connect personally.
   Facial expressions are observable albeit they're less defined due to size constraints, lighting variations, camera quality, and each participant's ability to soften an image.

Depending on camera angle and proximity, arm movement may be observable. Be mindful of making too many or too few gestures and of how big those gestures are.

If you type during meetings, only do so if you can type without looking at the keyboard. Otherwise it can be distracting and disrespectful.

If you work standing, stand still during the meeting. Movements appear exaggerated when someone's standing, and too much movement is distracting and disrespectful.

5. Appearance

Clothing and grooming should be professional based on your company's norms. Rather than let everyone guess, leaders should decide and communicate a dress code for video meetings. Although it is unlikely that personal grooming will be mentioned in any office memo, it is important to comb your hair and wear clothing that isn't wrinkled just as you would if you were going into the office.

Your lighting, camera angles, and background are part of your appearance. Some companies provide backgrounds while others set guidelines. Microsoft Teams Together Mode places participants in a shared background so it looks like you're sitting in the same room. One shared background removes the distraction of everyone's unique environment.

Your background communicates things about you and can add to or detract from your communications. Is your face lit up? Is there sun glare? Is the room messy? Are you in front of a completely blank wall? Your background tells a story about you. Consider blurring your background to neutralize it. Ideally backgrounds should be simple and plain. Think about sitting in a conference room. Except for an occasional picture, the walls are blank.

Cautions

- Zoom is an often-overused medium.
- We tend to schedule video meetings when other collaboration modalities may be better.
- Zoom fatigue caused by staring directly at a camera without breaking eye contact gets intense.
- The temptation to multitask is strong.
- Virtual social events may not be relaxing for all.
- Sessions without breaks are exhausting.

LIVE FACE-TO-FACE MEETINGS

Before 2020, when organizations had to pivot to full-time remote work, face-to-face meetings were as pervasive as email. Days were filled with back-to-back meetings and a steady flow of emails. Some people complained meetings sucked up their time. Others complained about the excessive time spent writing and responding to emails. Meetings were generally limited to business hours, although that sometimes made for long days. Emails were not limited to business hours.

Like automatically being added to email distributions, it is all too common for people to attend meetings without questioning who should attend or whether the meeting needs to take place at all.

Meetings include all the components of collaboration. The ability to be with someone in the same room allows you to use all your senses too. The most important is visual. Live, face-to-face collaboration brings a rich opportunity to build interpersonal glue with the least amount of miscommunication—at least compared to the other collaboration modalities.

The biggest problem with meetings is that they tend to be costly. Doodle's 2019 study of over 65,000 professionals found that pointless meetings cost their companies over $541 billion in 2019.[1] However, the same study found that 76 percent of professionals prefer face-to-face meetings to video meetings or calls.

Julie was coaching the newly promoted COO of a multi-hospital medical center. The COO needed help leading a large team, addressing morale problems, and managing stress. At one of their meetings she said, "This is the only meeting in my week that is not double booked, and I never cancel." She showed Julie her calendar. Julie saw every time slot filled with one to three meetings. Knowing the stress that occurs from overcommitment and the impact on teams when leaders don't show at meetings, Julie recommended starting with a *meeting inventory.* The goal was reducing all double and triple bookings, freeing time to think, decreasing stress, and increasing morale. A meeting inventory examines the purpose and effectiveness of every meeting. Together Julie and her client painstakingly evaluated each meeting.

1. Does she own the meeting?
2. Does she generally attend or cancel meetings she owns?

3. If she owns and attends, is the meeting the most efficient way to accomplish the group's goals?

   a. If yes, could they be shorter or less frequent?
   b. If yes, do all the people who are invited need to be there?
   c. If yes, could someone else own the meeting?
   d. If no, what other collaboration method would be more efficient?
   e. If no, is collaboration needed on this topic at all?
   f. Is there a clear purpose for the meeting? If yes, what is it? If no, it needs to be defined.

4. If she owns and regularly cancels, are there any consequences of canceling a meeting?

   a. If yes, what are they?
   b. If no, why keep it?

5. If she doesn't own but attends, does she really need to attend?

   a. If yes, what is her relationship to the person who owns the meeting? Is it because she thinks she should attend or because others expect her there?
   b. If no, why does she go, and what would be consequences of being taken off the meeting invite list?

6. If she doesn't own and doesn't attend, why is it on her calendar?

   a. If it's someone on her team, how can she work with that person to evaluate the meeting purpose, participant list, and frequency and then empower him or her to make changes?
   b. If it's owned by someone outside her department, what would happen if she asked the meeting owner to take her off the invite list?

As a result of the meeting inventory, with two exceptions she got rid of all double and triple bookings. There were two meetings that she assigned to one of her direct reports and wanted to keep in on her calendar so she would get the meeting notes. She permanently canceled or decreased frequency, time allotment, or attendees for most of the other meetings that she owned. For the meetings that her team owned, she partnered with them to decrease the number, frequency, and attendees.

For the meetings that were owned by people outside her team, she politely uninvited herself to three of them.

It took some time for the above transition. The long-term benefit of this exercise was defining the purpose of each meeting, including coming up with accurate meeting names that kept the meetings focused. The Carlson Project Monday Update Meeting was to share progress from the week before and identify deliverables for the coming week. It was not time to discuss budget problems with the IT Department—that was for the Tuesday Budget Meeting, which was good news for the Carlson folks. They were now free from 10 to 11 a.m. every Tuesday.

Opportunities for Use

- people want to meet, are co-located, and are free to get together
- building interpersonal glue
- brainstorming and complex discussions
- addressing negative, contentious, or problematic matters
providing personal or development feedback

Guidelines for Use

- Ask yourself if you need to meet.
- Plan, plan, plan.
- Include five to ten minutes of pre-meeting for building interpersonal glue.
- See to it that everyone is either on video or off video if possible.
- Keep it as short as possible.
- For meetings over sixty minutes, take a break.
- For meetings sixty minutes or shorter, allow a five-minute break for every twenty-five minutes of meeting time.

Cautions

- Meeting time is costly.
- People default to meetings when other collaboration methods may be more efficient.
- Meetings can be exhausting.
- Without structure, it's easy to get off track.

HYBRID MEETINGS

Hybrid meetings include participants sitting in the same room with a live stream of participants joining remotely. While at first look these might seem the best of both worlds, they are quite challenging to facilitate or participate in. These challenges appeared in 2021 as organizations returned to in-person meetings at different rates. While video meetings had their challenges and disadvantages, at least everyone was on a level playing field. Everyone appeared to be the same size, everyone faced the same way, no one was able to look directly at anyone else, and the strain of sitting in front of a computer screen impacted each participant.

It takes energy to bridge in-office participants sitting in one room with remote participants sitting in separate rooms. Attending a hybrid meeting on automatic pilot using old practices won't work. Leaders and team members need to be intentional to bridge the gap.

Successfully joining participants in different locations includes addressing various challenges. Here are some things to keep in mind:

- Technology: The tools you use make a difference. Allotting funds to modernize screens, linkages, microphones, and collaboration tools will help the integration. Participants need to be trained on the technology.
- Facilitators and participants need to be trained on best practices to maximize inclusive collaboration.
- Teams should set guidelines for participation and hold to those guidelines. Foster ways to encourage interaction between participants across locations.
- Remember that in-office participants tend to dominate over remote participants. This means remote participants need to assert themselves and in-office participants need to be solicitous of remote teammates.
- Review the agenda and consider if a virtual meeting might be a more effective mode for collaboration.
- Plan.

With an understanding of the different modes of collaboration, your team and you will be aligned on their use. We recommend generating a team charter to set guidelines for respectful collaboration such as which modality to use when and the expected response times for each modality to maximize engagement and productivity.

Chapter Eleven

Compassion

Compassion is about caring for others as individuals.

In chapter 6 we discussed what caring for an organization at large looks like. In chapter 9 we looked at communication from the point of view of the speaker: What do *you* want to say? How should *you* speak, sound, and look to be heard? In chapter 10 we explored connections between *you* and *others*. What do you and others need to get work done together? How do you and others feel about the team?

Compassion is about the *other*. Just one person at a time. What does the other person need? What does the other person have to say? How is the other person feeling? Is the other person stressed? Does the other person feel heard?

Caring for others requires empathy and compassion. They are frequently used as synonyms, but *Psychology Today* differentiates them.

- Empathy means sharing another person's emotions.
- Compassion is more engaged than simple empathy because it also involves an active desire to relieve the other person's suffering.[1]

Leaders showing empathy have a competitive advantage.[2] The Businessolver State of Workplace Empathy Study, a large multiyear study, found 72 percent of leaders believe empathy drives motivation and 84 percent of leaders think empathy drives better outcomes, but only 25 percent of employees feel the empathy they get from their leaders is sufficient.[3]

What this study suggests is that while leaders think empathy is important, they're not good at showing it.

If empathy means sharing another person's emotions, the question is *how*. Sharing someone else's emotions is accomplished by listening and making them feel heard. Listening and making somebody feel heard are not the same thing. The latter requires active listening, a multifunction tool that a leader can use to facilitate growth too. It is also a prime tool to convey empathy and the first step in demonstrating compassion. The power of helping someone feel heard is remarkable. If you ask someone to describe what it feels like to be heard, truly heard, you often hear words like *empowered, weightless, understood, less alone, relieved, less stressed*.

Stress is a part of everyone's lives, and it increased at the start of the COVID pandemic. Many things contributed to the increase including loneliness, a sense of being disconnected, increased work, decreased opportunities for activities, and the lack of boundaries between work and home. Without anywhere to go, employees were leaning on their managers more than ever. What did they need? Empathy and compassion. The problem was that leaders didn't feel equipped to handle listening to the pain and challenges. Julie heard comments like, "This is above my paygrade," "I can't believe how hard this is," "I'm exhausted by listening," "I don't know what to do with what I'm hearing." Julie's response was, "Listening is hard and exhausting." What should you do? Help employees feel heard.

Simple? Yes. Easy? No.

To help know when someone feels heard, Julie suggests her clients picture the other person holding an unknotted and overinflated balloon. As they speak, air slowly comes out of the balloon. Once all the air is out of the balloon, they will feel heard. Then they will feel your empathy.

Listening is one of the most powerful, underutilized leadership tools. It takes intentionality and practice to cultivate active listening. Given its effectiveness and low cost, detailed suggestions will never be overkill. But just saying, "How are you?" and accepting "Fine" as the response won't build feelings of empathy. Let's look at two ways to be intentional and to keep your employees talking until all the air is out of the balloon.

Acknowledgment is

* reflecting what the person is saying
* saying back the essential meaning, content, or feelings
* paraphrasing, summarizing, or checking your perceptions
* testing to ensure what you heard is accurate
* helping the speaker get clear
* capturing and reflecting the gist of the speaker's feelings

Acknowledgment is not

* being critical or judgmental
* telling someone how to feel (for example, "You shouldn't be upset.")
* telling a person what to do

If someone tells you, "I am upset because my work has not been up to par lately. Absolutely nothing is going well," your first response should not be, "Don't be upset, you're fine." That response will only shut the person up and create distance from you. It won't make the person experience empathy or compassion. Instead try, "Seems that you're feeling off from your normal performance." Then stop talking. We promise, the other person will keep talking.

Inquiring is

* asking open-ended questions that don't have a specific answer and allow freedom of response
* asking closed-ended questions that seek specific data
* asking pointed or probing questions
* testing assumptions

Inquiring is not

* asking rhetorical questions that are judgments in disguise
* asking leading questions that are assertions in disguise

If you want to shut a person up, convince him or her you don't listen and fuel his or her negativity. Say things like, "Why would you ever want to do that?" or "Don't you think you overreacted?"

If you want to keep a person talking, say something like, "What happened at the meeting that caused you to become quiet?" It will fuel positivity and let the person feel your empathy.

Another way to remember that empathy involves more listening than speaking is to picture your face. You have two ears but only one mouth. Show empathy by listening twice as much as you speak.

Here are ways you can demonstrate empathy through active listening.

- Review the guidance in chapter 8 with the idea of exploring ways to amplify your active listening. The combination of connecting and active listening is an excellent recipe for conveying compassion.
- When someone is in the office:
  - Randomly stop by his or her desk or stop walking if you pass in the hall, stop looking at your phone, and ask, "How are you?" and say it like you mean it. It's a powerful question. Please use it. But when the person says, "Fine," and we promise you he or she will, remember your two ears and start with active listening.
  - Depending on your comfort zone and the degree of interpersonal glue between you, ask another question such as "How was your weekend?" or "How is the challenging client?" Regardless of what the answer, follow up with another question or reflection. Do this as necessary until all the air is out of the person's balloon.

Caution: In addition to your ears, use your two eyes. If you see the person is busy with something else, find another time. Julie was working with a principal at an advertising firm. His team felt he was distant and never around, didn't care about them, and was clueless about how hard they worked. When he heard this feedback, he was surprised. He didn't reach out to them when they were busy because he thought he would be bothering them. So here was his challenge. On one hand, he needed to convey empathy and compassion, on the other, he needed to respect their busy time. Julie made a radical suggestion: Walk up to someone's desk, and rather than just ask "How are you?" start with "I'm wondering how you are. Are you busy and is this a good time to chat?" It was radical because he'd never thought of asking if it was a good time or that people might want to chat even if they looked busy. Julie suggested he make a note of when different people were busy. If you know advertising firms, you know that everyone is always busy. It's just a question of how busy. Once he knew people's patterns, he knew when he could stop by. He was surprised by the overwhelming feedback. Merely asking his employees, "Are you busy?" made them feel heard; that is, he had acknowledged they were busy, so they felt his empathy and told him how much they appreciated his concern.

- **Call them on the phone** if someone is working remotely. If he or she picks up, follow the same guidelines as you would if you were stopping by in the office. If the person doesn't pick up, leave a voice message that says, "I'm wondering how you are. Please call me back and let me know a good time to chat." Or just call back at another time. Your team may not be used to answering unscheduled calls. We'd suggest you frame unscheduled calls as virtual drop-bys.
- **Scheduled check-ins or team meetings**, whether virtual or in person, are times to convey empathy and compassion with active listening. Consider having a pre-meeting at the start of every check-in or team meeting that includes you actively listening. Pre-meetings are for nonwork-related connections. Your team experiences your compassion when you give time for these conversations. You can try versions of "What's up?" or "How are you?" or more creative ways to get them talking such as, "What's been taking up space in your head recently?" "What have you done that's fun recently?" or "What is something you're proud of this week?"
- **Surveys or questionnaires** show empathy because you are saying, "We want to hear what you have to say." You will convey empathy just by creating the survey. Collecting and using accurate data are difficult due to questions of confidentiality, possible misinterpretation, inaccurate analysis, or incomplete write up, but it's worth the effort. Collecting data is the first step of active listening. But note: Not sharing the results is akin to not listening and will likely breed distrust. Sharing the results is how you help the participants feel heard.
- **Focus groups** also show empathy. By nature, they indicate, "We want to hear what you have to say." They can be quite powerful, but they also have the same challenges as surveys and questionnaires. Confidentiality and creating a safe space for people to speak are

especially important. Focus groups are usually conducted by outside consultants because an external, neutral facilitator can create a comfortable place for people to speak and feel heard.

- **Follow-up surveys, questionnaires, or focus groups** with in-person, hybrid, or all-remote town halls to reflect on, synthesize, and summarize the feedback. In other words, actively listen so people feel heard. Soliciting questions in advance or during town halls also conveys empathy through your desire to listen. Sometimes leaders are afraid to take questions, as there may be things that can't be shared. Being open to questions conveys caring. Telling someone you can't share a specific answer conveys honesty. Taken together, they express empathy.

Northwell, a large healthcare provider, surveyed and formed focus groups to enable employees to be heard about their hybrid work structure. They then took the data and encouraged each team to generate personalized schedules that would work for each individual and the team. The focus groups expressed empathy, and the subsequent actions conveyed compassion.[4]

After the air is out of the balloon, your employee will feel your empathy. Now it's time to relieve the pain and do something. Here are some ways to act in a compassionate manner:

- **Express appreciation and praise.** One way of expressing compassion is letting someone know you appreciate them. As with listening and acknowledging, expressing appreciation goes a long way. And while you're at it, throw in some praise. Chapter 9 includes strategies for delivering appreciation and praise.
- **Ask "How can I help?"** You may be able to provide the support yourself or you may need to seek out other resources. Or you may not be able to do anything other than listen and acknowledge. Leaders sometimes are afraid to ask because they think that the person will ask for something they cannot deliver. If that's truly the case, what you can give beyond listening is honesty. Be transparent. Team members will respect you.
- **Provide them with the leadership style they need.** Tailoring leadership to individual needs is the premise of the situational leadership model. Situational leadership requires leaders to demonstrate effec-

tiveness and compassion by adapting what they give to individuals based on their individual needs. Employees may need support from you that's delivered in one of four ways: (1) telling, directing, or guiding; (2) selling, coaching, or explaining; (3) participating, facilitating, or collaborating; or (4) delegating, empowering, or monitoring. There are comprehensive courses available on situational leadership. We highly recommend taking one of them.

- **Support boundaries and work–life balance.** Hybrid work by nature blends working from home with working in the office. Combine that with technology that is always available, and it is easy for there to be no boundaries between work and home. Without boundaries, work spills over into everything. For starters, consider your own work habits. Julie has worked with many leaders who say, "I may work late and on weekends, but I don't expect my team to." Even if you say something like this, when you model the opposite, you're conveying the expectation that your team should be working 24/7 too. Leaders convey compassion by setting limits even if the employee doesn't request them or complain. Supporting boundaries with intentionality entails observing each of your team member's work habits. If your employees are not setting their own boundaries, share your observation and help them establish them.

Julie worked with a team at a fast-paced, high-pressure start-up with a hybrid policy that gave all employees "full flexibility" if they got their work done. The founder was a pleasant guy who worked all the time. His team ended up interpreting *full flexibility* as work full-time and then some. He was surprised when people quit and to hear people were stressed and miserable. He thought he was quite respectful with such a lenient hybrid policy. What he missed was that his team felt he was out of touch and didn't understand the impact of his behavior on them. He then met with each team member and asked about their workload; their preferences for how, where, and when to work; and their personal priorities and commitments. Morale started to change just with him expressing empathy and listening. He then went on to help everyone create his or her own boundaries. He continues to reinforce his message to his employees, including admitting he needs to work on creating his own boundaries.

- **Provide support for physical and mental illness.** Employees who are sick with observable ailments such as the flu are easy to spot. In cases like this, showing empathy and providing support is relatively easy. Sick employees may need their remote schedule altered or time off for doctor's appointments for recovery. But many physical illnesses are not observable and may, in fact, be a manifestation of mental health issues. People who are under stress may have physical manifestations such as insomnia, lack of or excessive appetite, general physical ailments, headaches, stomach aches, or heart arrythmias. There may be emotional manifestations such as anxiety, depression, low energy, no interest in pleasurable activities, or difficulty concentrating. Leaders cannot be expected to diagnosis illnesses, but they can be attentive to employees' behavior. They can watch for changes. Are they exhibiting decreased productivity? Unusual mistakes? Missed deadlines? Increased tardiness? Lethargy? Argumentativeness? Moodiness? Distractedness? If you notice any of these changes in your employees, you can be an active listener and express compassion. Ask them how they are. Ask them how you can help. Provide resources. Some of Julie's clients exhaust themselves because they spend a lot of time listening and feel a responsibility to do something when they don't know what to do. Remember: Listening is doing something. A referral to a therapist may be called for. Stress can come from many places outside of work.
- **Address burnout.** Burnout is a psychological condition that results from chronic stress. The three key dimensions of this response are overwhelming exhaustion, feelings of cynicism and detachment, and a sense of ineffectiveness and lack of accomplishment. How do you know if someone is burned out? Start with asking yourself, "Is he or she acting differently?" If the answer is yes, simply ask the person if he or she is burned out. Look for any of these behaviors in your employees:

  o They don't put in effort like they used to.
  o They don't seem excited about work.
  o Their performance is down.
  o They look or complain about being exhausted.
  o They have physical problems such as insomnia, headaches, arrythmias, or stomach problems.

You can help them alleviate symptoms like these by providing resources such as yoga, exercise classes, stress-management training, subsidized gym memberships, and so on. But what about the causes of burnout? A Gallop study[5] of 7,500 employees found the top five reasons for burnout are the following:

1. Unfair treatment at work—Consider your hybrid policy. Is it fair? Are employees treated equally?
2. Unmanageable workload—Are you aware of each person's workload? Do you check in to ask if it's too much or too little? Do you have enough staff so that people have manageable workloads?
3. Lack of role clarity—Does each person know what he or she is expected to do? What are his or her roles and responsibilities?
4. Unreasonable time constraints—Can the work be done within work hours? Are there always tight deadlines?
5. Lack of communication and support—Do you give information on a regular basis for your team to do their job and feel engaged? Do you know what support they need and provide it?

Demonstrating compassion to address burnout requires you to reflect on your work environment and modify the work as needed. And if you yourself are experiencing burnout, see chapter 15.

○ **Always respond to mistakes in a calm and respectful way.** Most people when they make a mistake feel bad for any of several reasons. They may have high standards and feel disappointed in themselves. Or they don't want to let you down. Maybe they fear they should have been more careful, and they believe the mistake could have been prevented. Perhaps they're ashamed. And worst of all, they're probably afraid you'll get mad. Of course, people don't make mistakes on purpose, so this is one of those times when they need compassion and understanding. A study by Google found safe team environments where people weren't afraid to make mistakes were also the highest functioning.[6]

There are a lot of ways to express empathy and compassion. Doing so will take time out of your already busy schedule, but remember: It is part of your job, and it's okay to start small.

Chapter Twelve

Coaching

Chapter 11 highlighted the importance of compassionate leadership. Perhaps the most powerful way to demonstrate compassion and enhance satisfaction is committing to employees' development. How do leaders facilitate growth and development? Coach each employee.

Every human wants to grow; people generally view their jobs as the place that growth can occur. This is especially true as one can measure growth via a promotion, additional responsibilities, a team to manage, leading accounts, not to mention getting a raise. On one hand, all people are responsible for their own career. On the other, bosses have a responsibility in supporting or facilitating growth.

As will be discussed in section IV, leaders need to be conscious of giving the same advancement opportunities to all. Think about these guidelines as "one size fits all" with respect to your support. Equal treatment of team members is challenging when everyone works solely in the office, or everyone works remotely. It is harder in a hybrid work environment. Once again, intentionality is required to maintain equity. And complementing the "one size fits all" is "one size fits one;" that is supporting and addressing everyone's strengths, development areas, career aspirations, opportunities for success, and so on.

Sounds like a lot to do. It is. We understand that maximizing productivity is one of your priorities and we will discuss that in section III. However, coaching everyone will facilitate growth, and maximize productivity. Leading your team *and* each individual member *is* your job. Many leaders are experiencing the "hybrid paradox." While in-person connection is becoming less frequent, coaching people is more important than ever. The best leaders allocate more leadership time to team management and coaching.[1]

Here are five things you can do to be an effective coach:

1. Be accessible.
2. Set goals.
3. Give feedback.
4. Facilitate growth with active listening.
5. Provide resources.

BE ACCESSIBLE

In the past, leaders could be accessible by relying on random walks through the hall to coach and connect with their direct reports. Not so now. Employees are not necessarily in the office at all, or on the same day, or on random days, or are booked eight hours straight thanks to our new protocol of scheduling everything. Remember when you could make a call without scheduling it? Leaders can no longer leave coaching and connection to chance.

With respect to accessibility, "one size fits all" means all employees need equal access to leaders. While equity is important, the reality in a hybrid work world is that "one size fits one" means different blends of accessibility may be necessary. There are two types of accessibility for one-on-one coaching.

1) Schedule meetings to occur at a regular interval. Ideally, they are both short-term, such as check-ins, and long-term, such as performance reviews. As these are planned, and assuming the employee is in the office sometimes, it's most effective to hold these meetings face to face. If in-office meetings are not possible, video meetings are preferred, in that documents can be shared live in the meeting.

Short-term check-ins should be 15 to 60-minute weekly or bi-weekly meetings. Whatever cadence you set, it is important to keep the meeting. A sure way to demotivate an employee is to reschedule a one-on-one meeting often, or worse, cancel the meetings. Employees perceive canceled or rescheduled meetings as an indicator that their boss doesn't care about them and is not invested in their growth.

Employees and bosses should have joint ownership of these meetings. Specifically, each person has the responsibility to set a meeting agenda, including update and discussion items. We recommend keeping some notes after each meeting. They do not have to be lengthy, but with regular progress notes, there will be much less work compiling quarterly, bi-annually, or annual reviews. Done right, you will have given each employee timely feedback, such that when reviews occur, there is not much to talk about, and you can just go out for coffee.

2) Unplanned coaching occurs on an irregular basis. These unplanned coaching moments can happen serendipitously, at the metaphoric water cooler, walking over to someone's desk, calling someone (yes, you can call someone without scheduling it, and the person may answer the call), or responding in a timely way to emails and instant messages. An open-door policy works well for in-office workers who learn cues to show you're available. If they are on the phone or have their chair turned away, don't come in. If they are on the computer and facing the door, come on in. This doesn't work for people working remotely. Creative alternatives are now required.

The team of one of our clients was complaining that their boss was not available. These complaints came from those people working in the office as well as people working remotely. We collected feedback from the team and it appeared that while the boss said there was an open-door policy, in fact he generally kept his door closed and rarely responded to emails or instant messages in a timely manner. The staff ended up spending a lot of time off-task complaining to each other about how their work was impacted by his non-responsiveness. When we discussed these complaints with the boss, he said that he was quite busy with his "work." We reminded him that being accessible, coaching, and providing feedback were his job. We then explored his schedule and combined it with the needs of the team. It was agreed that the busiest time when employees would be looking to connect with the boss was between 12 and 1 p.m. He agreed to daily "open office hours." He kept a live video stream open and shared the link with everyone while also keeping his door open. This enabled people to walk in, simultaneously with remote workers dialing in making ad hoc meetings possible.

So, too, you can stop by someone's desk, you can randomly call someone, and expect the person to pick up. Assuming he or she is not in a meeting. This does require a team-wide agreement for connecting. We call this a "team charter." Team charters will be discussed in length in the chapter on productivity.

As for asynchronous communication, including email and IM, accessibility means timely responsiveness. One way to determine if your team thinks you respond to emails in a timely manner is simply to ask them what they need from you. Recognize that if you're not responding in a timely manner, you are breeding bad will, frustration, and impaired productivity. Consider re-adjusting your priorities. Responding to your team should be high on the list.

For equity's sake, although some people may get more unplanned coaching and others may get more planned coaching, in the end, leaders should be equally accessible to their entire team.

Now that we've established that you should be accessible, let's explore some essentials when coaching your team.

One size fits all: You need to coach everyone.

One size fits one: Everyone's coaching will be tailored to their needs.

SET GOALS

Goal-setting conversations typically happen during quarterly, semi-annual, or annual reviews. Ideally, these goals will stay top of mind throughout the year. This will ensure progress is being made to reach them.

The beginning step when coaching individuals is identifying where they would like to go. What are their aspirations? What are areas they would like to develop? What does growth look like for them? The more you use a structure to identify your goals and steps to achieve them, the greater probability you will have in accomplishing them. And utilizing a framework can help even more. If you search the Internet for "goal setting," the most common framework is generating SMART goals. George Doran gets credit for the acronym.[2] Doran was a consultant and former Director of Corporate Planning for Washington Water Power Company who published a paper about SMART goals in 1981. For the past 40+ years, his concept has been used prolifically, including by people such as self-improvement "guru" Anthony Robbins. It has staying power because it is a simple, but robust framework to clarify goals, evaluate them, and set a path to achieve them.

As employees should own their careers, and it is a leader's job to coach them in meeting their goals, it is recommended that employees start with identifying their specific goals. Simultaneously, as their boss, you can also identify goals for them. The next step would be to meet with them and look at the goals from the lens of SMART goals. It is not unusual for there to be a discrepancy between an employee's goals and the boss's goals for the employee. It will be imperative to align the two.

SMART Goal Framework

Specific: Think who, what, where, when, and how. If you can answer all these interrogatives with a word or phrase, chances are good that it is a specific goal. Goals should be observable behaviors. Thoughts and feelings are not observable behaviors. A goal of "happiness" is far from specific. If you can see it, chances are it is specific. "Vice President of Marketing" is a specific goal.

Measurable: Again, if it is an observable behavior, it will be measurable. For example: How many projects will you complete? How much new work will you take on? What are the evaluative criteria that determine success with what you've taken on?

Attainable: What do you have that can help you reach your goals? If you don't have it already, what else will you need to attain your goal? For example, if you want to become a manager, you will need to manage people. If you want to run the project, you need to learn project management software. If you want to be promoted, you need to complete a certain number of acquisitions, or sales, or placements in major media outlets.

Realistic: Can you meet the goals? Is it realistic that there are people in need of a manager, and that you can qualify to manage them? Is there room in the budget to get extra headcount? Is there project management training that is available to you, and if not, do you have the funds and time to complete the class? Do you have the knowledge and resources to complete the acquisitions, sales, or placements you desire?

Timely: How much time will it take to meet the goal? As Stephen R. Covey said, "Start with the end in mind." That is, once you have identified your goal, set a date to complete it. Then identify the steps to get there and see if time allotted for each step will allow you to reach your goal. Don't forget to allow time for snafus. The military relies heavily on a concept called backplanning: You determine the target date for completion and then work backward from that date to determine how much time is needed to complete the task.

GIVE FEEDBACK

As Warren Buffet said, "Honesty is a very expensive gift; just don't expect it from cheap people."[3] The best leaders are not cheap. They provide regular candid, honest feedback. Feedback is a gift. Your employees should cherish it.

Giving feedback once a year during a review covers the past. That is not always helpful feedback, as it is given after the event has occurred. Share feedback in real time, giving employees the opportunity to modify their behavior if needed, or get validated to continue doing the correct thing they had been doing. A more effective feedback strategy is using the short-term practices for being accessible such as regular check-ins, open doors, and ad hoc coaching. Many clients have come to realize that annual feedback is expensive, time-consuming, and not all that effective. They are moving toward a model requiring weekly, or even daily, feedback.

One of Julie's clients realized that their performance review process was not effective. This came to a head at a training session when one of the participants told the trainer that for the past two years, they have included comments about Mickey and Minnie Mouse in their performance review. They wondered whether anyone would catch it. For two consecutive years nobody noticed. It brought home the fact that people spent time writing performance reviews, yet no one was reading them much less using them to help somebody's career. The organization switched to a "Start, stop, continue" feedback model. Leaders were instructed to provide weekly feedback including specific things that the employee should stop doing, new things employees should start doing, and current behaviors to maintain.

This model aligns with our recommendation that giving frequent and small bits of feedback is the most beneficial type of coaching. Acknowledge the behavior as close to when it was demonstrated. That includes telling employees what they did right ("Continue"), what they did wrong or should no longer do ("Stop"), and what their next short-term goal is ("Start").

Consider these adages as a guide to giving feedback:

"Catch them doing something right." In the moment, praise them and tell them it's right. It will make them feel good and know what to keep doing.

"Strike while the iron is hot." When you see someone doing something they shouldn't be doing, or not doing something they should be doing, let them know. Then.

"Praise publicly. Criticize privately." If you have something positive to say, feel free to say it in front of others. If you are sharing negative feedback, do so privately.

FACILITATE GROWTH WITH ACTIVE LISTENING

While you're giving gifts, listening is a gift that is cherished by all. It helps someone feel valued and is an effective coaching technique. Ask questions, rather than just deliver information. This Socratic give-and-take learning method helps people develop, and it helps you learn about them. In addition, the process of talking out loud increases ownership and following through on behavior. The same tool that is used to express compassion can be adapted and used to facilitate growth.

ACTIVE LISTENING

There are two types of active listening: a) Reflections are responses aimed to keep the person talking, including paraphrasing back, repeating back, saying *tell me more*, or even just nodding your head. And b) asking questions. There are two primary types of questions. Open-ended questions are narrative in nature and meant to keep the person talking through the problem. They begin with an interrogative such as who, what, when, where, why, or how. Closed-ended questions have a single answer: yes, no, or maybe. Hearing that, you ask an open-ended question and then listen. This process can help your employee solve problems and give you valuable insights about the employee's concerns, priorities, self-perceptions, and expectations.

PROVIDE RESOURCES

In concert with the above qualities, good coaching includes being a resource for your employees. Some of the things you can be a resource for include the following:

- **Recommendations:** Good leaders provide guidance and recommendations. They can be tangible such as how to solve a problem, getting resources, handling a conflict, how to make more with less, ways to be innovative, and so on. When working on the "Realistic" step in generating the SMART goals, a boss can be helpful. Or when discussing this week's challenges during check-ins, answer the direct questions or clarify deliverables. A simple way to find out what your direct report needs: Ask them.
- **Share strategy:** People want to be part of something big. Employees want to know the future direction of the organization. It helps with employee engagement and job satisfaction. Not to mention being able to do your job better. Share the big picture including what else is going on with the team, and with the organization at large. After all, if you were on Henry Ford's first assembly line, wouldn't you like to know that the metals you were bending each day were in fact the door handles? And the door handles were for the horseless carriage?
- **Mentor direct reports:** Mentoring entails sharing information, guidance, teaching and guiding someone's progress. This component of coaching is totally dedicated to the individual's career development. Discussions may center around goals that go beyond the one-year SMART goals. It is an opportunity to be a role model to discuss goals that aren't specific and may not be realistic. But reaching for the sky can be a motivator. Then acting as a coach, you can help them connect their pipe dreams to reality.
- **Mentor employees outside of your team:** You can also mentor people who are not on your team. Or partner with human resources to develop an organization-wide mentoring program. Julie has helped organizations build mentoring programs. A recipe for success: Obtain feedback about mentoring needs, define goals, generate equitable guidelines for pairing, establish the program specifics, and most importantly, train mentors and mentees on how to get what they want out of the program. Organizations that skip any of the above,

especially training, will have mentors who want to mentor, but don't know how to. And after two-six meetings, will stop meeting with their mentee.

- **Facilitate opportunities for visibility and advancement:** You can be a powerful resource for your employees by helping them make connections and be seen with people who are in positions of power or influence. Don't just tell them to show up at a meeting. Rather, help them craft a contribution or way to show off their skills. In addition, consider their goals, and what advancement would look like for them. This is something that should be "one size fits all" meaning everyone should benefit from your assistance. But also, "one size fits one" such that you the opportunities you provide meet the needs of each individual. In a hybrid world, it certainly takes intentionality, and perhaps creativity to facilitate visibility and advancement for all. Visibility is more powerful in the office. With planning and monitoring your teams in-office schedule, you can be mindful to facilitate opportunities. Remote opportunities are possible but require more structure. Perhaps you not only have the person join a more senior meeting, but also, give them an active role, speaking part, or even lead the meeting.
- **Networking:** In a hybrid world including people working at different times and in different places, networking is challenging. It may be within your team or with other teams. Consider making a "lunch buddy" system. That is a schedule to partner everyone up each week to have lunch. It can be a virtual or live lunch. The goal is just to get to know others. Or perhaps schedule mixers with other departments. Or "lunch and learns" with discussion groups are great ways to meet new people. Once again, be intentional about creating opportunities for your team to network with others.

Pick one *small* thing from above to start with.

And if you're unsure how to start being a coach, try two simple questions:

How are you doing?
How can I help?

Section III

MAKING HYBRID WORK

Section I took you through the steps your organization can take to create a hybrid workplace structure that aligns with your organization's values, business, and people. Once your hybrid workplace model has been created, it then falls on the leaders to guide employees in this hybrid world. Section II identified the 7 Cs of leadership required to engage employees. Engaged employees are necessary but not sufficient to maximize growth. Individual and company-wide growth entails becoming an employer of choice, hiring, and retaining talented employees and maximizing productivity. None of this is possible unless you take care of yourself.

This section pulls together enterprise obligations, each leader's responsibilities, and the right tools to take care of the individual leader, that is, you.

Chapter Thirteen

Boosting Productivity

Up to this point we have gone through the steps to build a dynamic, successful hybrid work environment: approaching work with intentionality, clarifying organizational values and needs, designing and implementing the hybrid model that's right for your organization, and becoming an inspirational leader. The next step for leaders is to boost productivity. This means

1. Clarify values and strategy.
2. Align values and strategy with organizational structure and performance management.
3. Connect performance management to individual productivity.
4. Create a team charter.

It's about connecting the dots.

One of Julie's clients was a large public relations firm with a culture of hard work, long hours, and demanding clients. It was an intense but generally fun place to work. The drive for creativity energized all members of the firm. Maximizing innovation had always been the core value. As such, members of the organization who were extremely creative but difficult, hostile, or demeaning were tolerated. And even promoted. There were a few people who quit because of being treated poorly.

With a desire to grow, the firm added a second core strategy: increase market share in two additional sectors. Commissions for new business were increased. Revenue did increase but so did turnover, as the environment became more competitive and less supportive. Offensive behavior was still tolerated. It was no longer a fun place to work. More and more people quit. The top line increased but the bottom line decreased. The chief human resource officer (CHRO) connected the dots for the partners. She told them if they prioritized individual innovation and sales over good behavior, bad behavior and turnover would continue. The bottom line would continue to suffer. After many in-depth and somewhat contentious conversations, the partners changed the core values and strategy to include design innovation, collaboration and respectful teamwork, and diverse growth. The CHRO convinced the partnership that for these changes to take place, the performance management and compensation system needed to change. After another series of challenging conversations, respectful teamwork was added as a component of how everyone was measured. The weighting of collaboration and respectful teamwork ratings was equal to that of design innovation and sales in determining salary increases and promotions. Within the next year, there were noticeable changes. There was less yelling, some difficult people were terminated, and turnover decreased. These changes were possible because the partners changed what got measured. Strong performance rests on the simple principle that "what gets measured gets done."[1] And they connected the dots: What was measured was with their new values and strategy. Let's walk through these steps for boosting productivity.

1. CLARIFY VALUES AND STRATEGY

Just as you examined your values and strategy to develop a hybrid work model that fit your organization, reflect on them and determine whether they reflect your productivity goals. You may need to further clarify your strategy to include boosting productivity along with your hybrid mode. This is not an easy task; it may require difficult conversations. Consider everything that impacts your business, brainstorming to identify all components and factors of importance: products, services, priorities, customers, revenue goals, pay structure, culture, talent, expectations for behavior, legal issues, growth model, work environment, diversity, equity, inclusion, and so on. Once you've generated an exhaustive list, break it down to simple guiding principles that ideally are not more than three sentences. Generating a mission, strategy, and value statement is an onerous task. We suggest you dedicate time and resources to making it a guiding force for your organization. Once these are defined, they can be a guiding light to drive all decisions.

2. ALIGN VALUES AND STRATEGY WITH ORGANIZATIONAL STRUCTURE AND PERFORMANCE MANAGEMENT

After clarifying your values and strategy, the next step is to align them with your performance management. Start with reviewing your organizational structure. Does it align with your end goal of maximizing productivity? Look at the job titles and job descriptions. Does the title represent the overall role within the team or department? Job titles and detailed job descriptions are crucial to effective performance management. The job description should include detailed roles and responsibilities, which in turn will be tied to ongoing deliverables and measuring performance.

As you consider your values in adapting the hybrid model that's best for your organization, have you also specified new behaviors that are expected and need to be measured? Here are new factors to measure in a hybrid work environment and add to your performance review system:

- **Face time**—What amount of in-office face time is expected to maximize performance? Is face time a commodity that matters? If so, define why.
- **Communication**—Is the employee proactively communicating with others? Are communications clear? Are the person's emails well written? Is the person a good presenter in remote meetings and/or live office meetings? Does the person communicate well in hybrid meetings?
- **Collaboration**—Does the person collaborate in the most effective way with others? Is the person respectful in meeting others' needs or work-style preferences? Does the person respect coworkers' time?

- **Connection**—Does the person strive to build effective working relationships? Does the person build relationships beyond structured meetings? Is the person engaged and pleasant to work with?
- **Reliability**—Is the person available when needed? Does he or she reliably meet coworkers' needs and deliverables? Does the person keep coworkers updated regarding when and where he or she is reachable? Does the person respond to others in a timely manner?
- **Equity and inclusion**—Does the person include all others as needed and treat others equally? Is the person respectful of everyone regardless of differences? Does the person interact with others based on what's needed and not based on who the person is?

So too with generating a mission and values statement, reviewing and rewriting job descriptions as necessary is an onerous task that requires extensive time and resources. Now that you have reviewed and modified roles, job descriptions, and responsibilities, consider if deliverables can be generated from the listed responsibilities.

3. CONNECT PERFORMANCE MANAGEMENT TO INDIVIDUAL PRODUCTIVITY

In parallel with reviewing job descriptions, review your performance management system to see if it aligns with core strategy and values. Once again, certain behaviors will be demonstrated only if they are included as part of evaluations. And ideally those behaviors will be tied to compensation and promotion. If teamwork is a value and included as part of the job description, but individuals are reviewed only as individual contributors, no one will be motivated to be a collaborative team member. If respecting others is a value, but hostile, difficult people are rewarded, they will continue to be offensive. Unfortunately, just telling people to be kind to coworkers doesn't change offensive behavior. And if mentoring others is a value, then someone's ability to teach or develop others needs to be evaluated.

A mission statement and clear job descriptions are only useful when they are communicated to others. With respect to maximizing performance, it begins when someone joins the organization and then should be continually reinforced. For those who are already part of the organization, take time to meet with them and review their role, responsibilities, and deliverables. It will move them to be productive, engaged team members. These are important meetings and should be taken seriously by managers and leaders. Hence in a hybrid world, conducting these performance management meetings in the office will convey priorities and seriousness.

Most organizations have annual or biannual performance reviews. They become opportunities to reflect on the past six or twelve months. As noted in chapter 12, feedback should be provided on a daily or weekly basis. When feedback has been provided regularly, a biannual or annual review summarizes what has already been communicated. When done right, these reviews are a discussion about the future too. Based on the past year, what has the employee done well, what should he or she keep on doing? What has the person done but should no longer do? And what should the person start doing? These reviews take a lot of time to write and then to review in feedback meetings, however they are essential to maximize productivity. Connect the dots: job requirements and feedback.

Giving negative feedback is challenging for many people. And many sugarcoat negative feedback because they feel bad or just want to avoid a difficult conversation. The problem is that without accurate feedback, an employee assumes everything is fine. What happens all too often with poor performers is that no one tells them there is a problem. They get average to above-average ratings, and their poor performance continues until their manager can't take it anymore and they are fired. At best, you lose employees who could have improved if given timely feedback. At worst, you get sued for wrongful termination.

Giving feedback about someone's performance is nothing to feel bad about. And it is not creative writing. You are sharing facts as indisputable as the reality that you are sitting on a chair and grass is usually green. Someone who fails to meet deliverables simply fails to meet deliverables—it's just a fact. Sometimes many people know the facts about others' poor performance except those who could do something about it—because no one told them. When the poor performer is the last person to receive the feedback, he or she put at a distinct disadvantage and is unable to demonstrate a desire and ability to improve. Someone who is having challenges with a hybrid schedule may not be aware that his or her work is suffering. If the person is not told, chances are nothing will change. However if the person is told and his or her manager asks how to help, a simple modification in schedule may alleviate the problem. Feedback is a gift. It is the manager's job to share feedback and provide support, training, and resources to help the employee. It is then the employee's job to make changes based on the feedback.

4. CREATE A TEAM CHARTER

Creating a team charter is an opportunity to capture team values and rules of engagement. As to taking these big concepts and building a living guide, it's all in the details.

Just as the organization started with defining its values, so too your team should consider its values. These will help determine what's included in the charter. Start with hybrid work principles and then establish guidelines for connecting, communicating, and collaborating with others.

Ask a lot of *whys*. The power of *why* is understanding underlying issues. Knowing the root causes can help create and drive a guideline.

The development process should include the team leader's recommendations, team input, and pain points. As part of it, create guidelines for engagement. Refer to the 7 Cs for issues that should be addressed in the team charter.

Here are examples of guidelines. Pick the ones that feel right for you and your team.

Hybrid Flexibility Principles

- Leader has responsibility to lead the team.
- The work, team as a whole, and individual team members all matter.
- We have deliverables to meet.
- Team cohesion matters.
- Individuals are all different.
- Let others know what your schedule is.
- Let others know how to best contact you.
- If your schedule changes, let others know one day in advance.
- Be reliable.
- Leader establishes schedule after considering work and individual needs.

Connection Guidelines

- Connecting should be a part of every day you are in the office.
- Remember that relationships matter. Be proactive in building relationships.
- When you're in the office, spend fifteen to sixty minutes walking around and casually speaking with others.
- When you're in the office, get out of your chair sometimes and walk around.
- All meetings should include five to ten minutes for nonwork discussion.
- Create weekly rituals such as Friday shout-outs (rotate team members and each week spend ten and fifteen minutes with everyone praising, acknowledging, or expressing thanks to that person in person or via email); have weekly, biweekly, or monthly in-person social events; hold weekly, biweekly, or monthly virtual social events; schedule virtual happy hours (held if possible during work hours so people don't feel they're a burden).
- Team meetings should be held on a regular basis to ensure continuity of connection; work with your team members for each project to determine frequency.
- Set guidelines for office days for people to be intentional about randomly going over to each other's desk or meet in the kitchen or the like.
- When working remotely, pick up the phone and call someone at least once a week.
- Create a spreadsheet pairing people up for virtual lunch or physically going out to eat.
- Create a social channel on Slack to share personal tidbits or arrange social events.

Collaboration Guidelines

- Review the guidelines for each collaboration modality covered in chapter 10 and tailor each set of guidelines for your team. Look at whiteboards, emails, IMs or texts, individual phone and conference calls, and all-video and hybrid meetings.

Respecting Each Other's Time

- Give people enough notice to complete a task.
- Don't demand an immediate response unless necessary.
- Don't make others rush because you didn't plan.
- If you stop by someone's office, ask if he or she has time to chat. If not, leave.
- If someone stops by your office and you're busy, give a time when you will not be busy.
- Schedule personal office hours and include a Zoom link on your shared calendar and a phone number so anyone can virtually stop by or call.

The above suggestions were taken from different team charters. Each team had its own process to create their charter, but identifying pain points first generally got to the *whys*. Then the team did some brainstorming. We encourage you to use different modes of connection to brainstorm, because they will breed different results—virtual, electronic, and in person. Create a charter committee to take these ideas and write them up or select one person to write up the charter. Once the charter has been written, begin the real work of living it. Without buy-in, it will fail. Realistically, people can't adapt to a twenty-point set of guidelines all at once. It's a good idea to prioritize your guidelines then hold sessions to discuss what the guidelines mean for each person and then have each person commit to one to three of the guidelines to start.

Putting it together, making hybrid work, and maximizing productivity are big accomplishments. They will happen one step at a time.

Chapter Fourteen

Becoming an Employer of Choice
Hiring, Onboarding, and Retention

What do we mean by "employer of choice"? Think of that company you aspire to work for. Perhaps the company has a truly great product, the leader is inspirational, or you know people who rave about how happy they are at work. Or maybe the company is known for its inclusive environment. An employer of choice has developed a solid reputation that probably hits on all of these qualities. An employer of choice also has developed an employee value proposition: a concise statement that messages to employees and prospects the company's vision for its workforce. A value proposition is more than just a list of total rewards: It is a statement that captures the essence of the work experience. Yes, the financial terms of an offer are important, but increasingly, candidates are looking for opportunities where there is career development—training, mentoring, and allyship. Ideally the employee value proposition reflects the organization's commitment to creating community, which in turn translates into employee loyalty.

Become an employer of choice, and you'll be able to hire good people and develop and retain them. Developing a loyal workforce is challenging in an employee-centric and transient workforce. Yet organizations need a solid core of contributors—individuals who know the company, work well together, and share a history. Employers of choice develop loyalty. How do you create a culture that hits on all these qualities?

HIRING

Start with *making a great first impression*. First impressions mean everything; don't let anyone try to convince you otherwise.

The first chance your organization gets at demonstrating culture is the recruitment and interview process. Think of the recruitment process as a marketing tool: a way to communicate a positive message about your organization, its products and services. The recruitment process should always be guided by the employee value proposition: what makes working at your organization different from (and better than) the competition.

That begins with the job posting. Beyond details about job description, job postings should be clear about where and when the work will be done. Clearly communicate the answer to the *where* question. Let applicants know whether there is a remote option, or whether they will be required to report to an office on a regular basis. Some candidates will determine whether to even apply to a position based on the answer to the *where* question. Make sure the organization's employee value proposition is part of the posting.

Next is the interview. A key piece of advice: Be kind to applicants. Interviewing is not a hazing. Recruiters' key goal is to find the best qualified candidates and convince them to accept an offer. But consider this: Every applicant who is not made an offer should feel a bit of disappointment. Unsuccessful applicants should walk away from the process thinking that they wished they'd had the opportunity to work for your organization because it sounds like such a great place to work.

How to convey this message? Every part of the organization's applicant screening and selection process should be intentional. Interviewers, not just recruiters, should know what to ask, and know what information needs to be conveyed about the organization and its approach to work. Good hires will be people whose interests, talents, and desired work arrangements align with the organization's culture and hybrid arrangement and its job requirements.

Interviewers should proactively explain the organization's approach to where work is expected to be performed. Applicants will ask this question. Flexjobs, a job posting network, advises applicants to ask a series of questions about an organization's hybrid work policy and advises applicants to understand what they are really signing up for.[1] Managers should be prepared to answer the same questions when they meet screened applicants. Answers to tough questions like "Can I start early and leave early to pick up my children from school?" should be at the ready, and should be presented in an honest, caring way. Most important, the answers to these questions should be consistent. If one manager endorses flexibility while another is reticent, applicants will walk away from the process thinking the organization's commitment to hybrid work can't be counted on.

Interviewers also should be prepared to explain how the organization supports its distributed workforce. A sincere answer to such a question requires thought and preparation. An answer to this question can truly differentiate an organization. Imagine the impression an organization can leave applicants when managers can explain how the organization has developed a training program for leaders to meet the challenges of managing a team that includes a remote and hybrid workforce. When an interviewer can explain that he or she has received training to identify and interrupt proximity bias so that he or she can better evaluate and develop all staff, regardless of where they may be working, that will convey to applicants that the organization is serious about making flexible work opportunities fair and inclusive.

The bottom line: Interviewers cannot just give lip service to the concept of flexible work. Their answers to the probing questions they will hear from applicants must be clear and provide details that demonstrate the organization's commitment to flexibility. Just as applicants practice answers to anticipated questions, interviewers must do the same. Hiring someone you hope will be okay with your hybrid policy is setting yourself up to be replacing the new candidate in a few months. Your goal: Find applicants who match the job and work arrangements.

Here are steps and questions that drive best practices:

1. What is your employee value statement?
2. Review job postings. Do the postings accurately answer the question: Where must the position be performed?
3. Train recruiters. Do recruiters have information regarding where the work in issue must be performed?

   a. Is there a remote option?
   b. What is the hybrid schedule?
   c. How does the organization support its flexible approach?
   d. How does the hybrid policy really work?
   e. What technology is used to support the hybrid approach?

4. Train managers. Are managers partnered with recruiters to align messaging?

   a. Can you not only describe the organization's hybrid work policy, but also explain how the policy supports your team's success?
   b. Are you prepared to explain why staff is expected to report to an office on a regular basis if that's the policy, and why those days in the office are essential to the team's work?
   c. Can you describe how the organization supports leaders so they can manage a distributed workforce?
   d. Can you describe why the organization's approach supports the business model?
   e. Are you able to ask questions about how team members interact and get to know one another, ideally with concrete examples?
   f. Are you prepared with examples of how employees have succeeded in balancing the demands of work with personal obligations?
   g. Can you explain how the organization measures success?
   h. Have you conducted mock interviews as part of the interview training program for managers? This is the best technique to give the leaders the skills they need.

ONBOARDING

Imagine this: You've spent four months going through the interview process. While you had two job offers, you made your choice based on the people you met. It's your first day. A Monday. You arrive in your office. There are a few people there, but no one on your team. You don't know where to sit, so you sit in the kitchen. And wait. No computer. No team. You wonder if you made a mistake.

Or imagine your first day is a Monday. But it's a work from home day. You turn on your personal computer. You're not even sure how to log into the company system, no less what your new email address is.

Or imagine your first day is a Monday. It's one of your work from home days. You do know how to log in and have an email address. But once you do, you learn that everyone else is in the office that day.

Or imagine your first day is a Monday. You have nothing to do and get told, "Enjoy the quiet. It won't be that way for long." Two weeks later, it's still quiet and you haven't met the team nor been put on any projects.

Hopefully you haven't experienced any of these. But we've heard many of these horror stories. At their worst, the experience conveys a culture that doesn't value people, and the new hire quits within the month.

Onboarding done right starts with understanding the new hire's needs, includes direct involvement from managers, connects stakeholders, and engages the entire team. It begins the day the person is hired and will continue for one to three months.

Best-in-class approaches to new employee orientation entail preparing leaders with the tools needed to make the new employee's onboarding experience a positive one. First, anticipate and ask the new hire what he or she needs on the first day of work. What about day two to ten? Days eleven to thirty? Needs fall into three categories: people, tools, and performance.

For the people factor, it's safe to assume the first thing any new hire will want to do is meet the team. As discussed in chapter 8, the connection chapter, interpersonal glue is crucial to build an engaged and productive team. If your organization now includes teams of remote and hybrid employees, the onboarding program will entail introducing the new hire to all stakeholders regardless of where and when they work. Creative ways to build connections may be required. The connection chapter also includes ideas you can incorporate into your onboarding program.

Day one: Start with yourself. Onboarding is a leader's opportunity for the new hire to experience you as a compassionate leader. Start with asking questions to get to know the new hire. After all, knowing his or her preferences for when and where to work will enable you to work out a hybrid schedule that will follow organizational and team guidelines, and enable the employee to be a productive member of the team. If you've sold the new team member on your approach to flexibility, initial meetings to lay out expectations about the when and where of work are critical. Don't be afraid to talk about the role of trust in the process. Not only trust between the subordinate and supervisor, but trust between members of the team. When a team member disappoints his or her peers by not keeping up with work, the entire team suffers.

Within a week of start date, meet with your new hire and discuss what onboarding for the next three months will look like. Share the company's mission, team values, big-picture goals, team processes, and performance expectations. What do you want the new hire to accomplish in three months? What are weekly or bi-weekly deliverables?

Then consider the view of the world from the new hire's perspective. Who are his or her stakeholders? Team? Peers? Outside departments? Support functions? Human Resources? Payroll? IT? ID? Create a list of all the people the new hire will engage with. And introduce them. Or build a mechanism for the relationships to flourish.

Mentor programs and buddy systems are essential for new team members who may be reporting to a workplace only some of the time (or not at all). Again, when a team of mentors receive training on how to best support new co-workers, the organization's messaging is consistent, and the mentors will know what to do and how to do it. Simply assigning a team member to serve as a new colleague's buddy is not adequate. The program should be more intentional and strategic. Make sure your mentors are trained and know what is expected of them in this role. If the organization also assigns a peer "buddy," training also is necessary.

Simultaneously with meeting people, new hires need tools. Tools include physical things such as a computer, monitor, phone, desk, and chair. Consider the tools that employees need for hybrid work. Does your organization compensate employees for at-home office equipment? Does the person need a camera for remote work? Does the person have sufficient bandwidth at home? Companies vary in what they pay for.

Tools also include getting payroll set up, signing up for benefits, learning the team filing system and passwords, getting access to software and data, getting a tour of the building. Hot spots include the restrooms, conference rooms, and office/seating options. And don't forget about the kitchen. Knowing that Thursday mornings are for team breakfasts is also a valuable tool to be given to new hires. They will then know that Thursday is a day to come into the office if they want free croissants.

Information is the critical tool. Client lists. Client's nuances. Project deliverables. Project history. Assets. Growth areas. Legacy information. Growth strategy. Office politics. Team alliances. Name of the person to call for travel. Team RACI chart. Email distribution lists. Standard meeting times.

Imagine how terrific it would be to receive all the information about how to work with your team on day one. One of our clients figured that out. It was the research and design division of a consumer product company. One of the departments was responsible for writing user manuals for the products. A new hire jokingly said to her boss, "I wish I got a manual for how this team works on my first day. It would have saved me a lot of headaches." Her boss approached us to help them write a team user manual. This manual was not the same as the company handbook. It included the minute details of the "tools" needed to work in that team.

Armed with the right tools and knowing the right people, puts new hires in good stead to succeed in the next step of onboarding: performance. Performance management starts with onboarding and blends into retaining talent.

Identify, Grow, and Develop Talent

Think of your organization's performance management program as the roadmap for identifying, developing, and retaining talent. Our focus is on the hybrid workplace and how flexible programs can both challenge the management team and, when thoughtfully developed, provide a compelling reason for talent to make a long-term commitment.

Once again, intentionality is key, and training is the bedrock. (See the appendix for training recommendations.)

First, there should be a consistent approach to performance measurement. Leaders should be unified in answering the question: "What does success look like?" How this is accomplished when leading a distributed workforce takes a concerted effort. That concerted effort begins with an actual program. Where an organization has committed to a flexible approach, the ability to fairly evaluate performance requires much more than an annual review with a bunch of questions and a numerical rating system. If that's what your organization relies on its time to take a strategic approach and deploy a meaningful process. Second is to develop a formal process that allows the organization to determine whether leaders are leading and individual contributors' efforts are fairly measured. We urge organizations to invest in developing tools that require formalized feedback more often than annually. And those tools should address not only traditional metrics—the timing and quality of deliverables—but also leadership skills such as attracting and retaining diverse employees and supporting DEI programs, developing future leaders, and developing other attributes of a good corporate citizen.

Leadership training should be intentional. Even if your organization does not have a structured program for identifying and grooming future leaders, there are ways to allow future leaders to hone their skills and develop a personal leadership style.

Leaders must identify opportunities to showcase their team members' talent. One way to accomplish this is to hand the mike over. Rotate speakers when you conduct team meetings. No one wants to listen to the same person all the time. One organization that Felice works with instituted a new protocol for their weekly leadership meeting. Instead of the CEO serving as the emcee each week, this task is rotated. The opportunity to orchestrate the leadership meeting is viewed by attendees as a great way to hone leadership skills, to dive into the material (presenters have to be much more prepared than attendees), and to learn more about each of the topics under discussion. Attendees pay more attention because they are curious to see how their colleague handles the opportunity, and because each leader approaches the topics differently. The CEO also sees team members in action. A win-win all around!

Modeling good leadership skills will lead to the development of future leaders. Training for leaders is critical to developing and retaining talent (see our discussion in the training chapter). Leadership assessment is an important part of an organization's performance management program. The need for leadership assessment tools is magnified in a hybrid work environment, where it is difficult to see leaders in action on a regular basis. We recommend that a robust assessment be made of leaders on a regular basis.

Many tools have been developed to develop and assess leaders. Here are a few:

- Utilize a leadership assessment tool that reflects the organization's culture. The tool can be developed in conjunction with the assistance of a consultant with expertise in this area.
- Develop a leadership training program where future leaders are identified and groomed.

- Utilize 360 tools to ensure that leaders are viewed not only by their leaders but by their team members.
- Identify specific skills required for promotion and reliable benchmarks for those skills.
- Ensure that the performance is fairly recognized with an equitable pay program.

RETENTION

Talent retention is key to longterm success.

Where an organization can boast of long-term employees, applicants listen up. In an era where there is no stigma to changing jobs regularly, people stop and listen when they learn of decades-long relationships in the workplace. When folks commit to a company for double-digit years, something good must be happening.

Retaining talent is important to every organization. A cadre of long-term contributors who know the organization's lore and customs sends an important message to applicants, employees, and customers. The challenge in a hybrid workplace is employee engagement. That's why developing the connective glue we've talked about is critical. Every leader shares responsibility for talent retention, and your organization's performance evaluation tool should reflect the importance of this goal.

Mentors can also make a difference, provide the interpersonal glue, and demonstrate the strength of your organization's culture. The potential role mentorship programs play in not just the first days at work, but throughout the work experience, is really heightened when the workforce is distributed. Whether the organization relies on peer mentors, or mentors who are more experienced and serve as professional guides, ensuring that new hires have an opportunity to develop individual relationships is critical when everyone is not together under one roof all the time. The most effective mentorship programs provide mentors with training.

The mentor and buddy systems should also be supplemented with attention to allyship. Whether your organization has formalized an allyship program, leaders can and should pay attention to this critical support network. Allyship is a critical ingredient to a successful DEI program and refers to the role of leaders to support and advocate others—particularly those who don't belong to the same identity groups. So for example, if you are a straight white female leader, being an ally to a gay black female on your team involves more than just informing your team member how to join an affinity group that your organization sponsors. Allyship requires learning about other identity groups and understanding the roadblocks they might face in the workplace. Once armed with this information an ally can then serve as a meaningful advocate. Good leaders will signal to new hires that they are committed to an ongoing effort to support racial equality early in the employment relationship. When BIPOC (Black, Indigenous, and people of color) colleagues see from the start that leaders are willing to serve as an advocate, this is an important step in creating an inclusive workplace.

Increasingly, public corporations are issuing annual diversity reports that highlight how the organization has fared in achieving a more diverse workforce. If these results are important to an organization's top line, leaders should be required to demonstrate that they contribute to this effort, and those leaders who are successful should be rewarded.

STAY INTERVIEWS

Understanding what motivates employees will help you meet their needs and build loyalty.

Developing a culture of loyalty is not easy. If this is something your organization is struggling with, a calculated response is necessary. Throwing goodies at employees like free food will not work. Learning why employees would want to stay requires an intentional approach. Understanding what makes the culture fail or succeed, typically requires a number of approaches, but most important, organizations need to hear from employees and learn what matters.

One approach is the stay interview. It is a good practice for organizations to have in place a protocol where managers can continually get a pulse on individuals and trends. The stay interview is a also an opportunity to determine whether the work experience is living up to the employee value statement. It's one thing to draft an ambitious view of the workplace; living up to the promise of the employee value statement is the difficult follow-on challenge.

Stay interview questions should be pointed:

- Do you have the tools you need to be successful? If so, what are they? If not, what do you need? What tools do you need to be successful?
- Are you supported by your supervisor?
- Are our benefits package sufficient?
- Do you feel included?
- Have you received adequate training to excel?
- Is our mentorship program effective?
- Has the organization created a community that is inclusive?

In addition to stay interviews, climate surveys are a very effective tool. The survey questions should home in on a wide array of issues, but most important, should elicit information that will inform leaders as to where they need to focus their efforts. The survey should address the organization's efforts to create an inclusive environment—the "I" in DEI. Often, this is the problem. When employees do not feel that they are an appreciated and recognized part of an organization they leave. Leaders managing hybrid and distributed teams cannot lose sight of the importance of ensuring that every individual feels a part of the whole. One word of caution: Before embarking on an employee climate survey, we recommend that you get help from an expert with experience crafting survey questions and assessing results.

Developing and retaining good leaders is the key to a hybrid workplace. Leaders create the institutional glue, employee by employee. When leaders embrace the 7 Cs and support the wellness of their team, they will create a culture of engagement.

Chapter Fifteen

Wellness and Mental Health

Up until this point, everything you have been reading has been about you taking care of your organization. Taking care of your teams. Dealing with your leadership challenges. But what about you?

If you're concerned about being selfish, the *New York Times* 7-Day Wellness Challenge reminds us that "self-care isn't selfish."[1] Every flight attendant will tell you, "Put your oxygen mask on first." This chapter is about putting your oxygen mask on first.

It is unreasonable to expect that there will be no challenges in your life. Challenges can be good, bad, or just hard. You cannot erase them, but you can manage them. Traffic is traffic. Difficult clients are difficult clients. Sick relatives are unfortunately sick relatives. An interesting but complex project is terrific. But it is challenging. Two-year-old children are delightful. They also require a lot of attention. Moving is exciting. It is also exhausting.

Mental health problems occur when your challenges are greater than your ability to manage them.

Let's look at hybrid work and its impact on you as an individual.

FLEXIBLE SCHEDULES

Imagine you wake up in the morning, look at the clock, and wonder what day it is. Are you working from home, in which case you can go for a run before work? Or are you working in the office? In which case you need to pack your gyms clothes in order stop at the gym on the way home tonight. Or worse, you get your days mixed up. You hit the snooze button and wake up thirty minutes later only to realize it was a day to go into the office. You get dressed, don't have time to stop at the coffee shop, rush your commute, and are late for your first meeting. First thing in the morning, and you're already stressed.

By definition, flexibility is one of the core components of hybrid work. Variability is the good news and the bad news. It's good in that you can manage your life and work holistically. It's bad because the variety of hybrid work requires new neural pathways in the brain for these daily changes. Daily changes take mental energy, which in turn add challenge each day. Change, challenges, and needing extra energy to function can add up to stress.

Action steps to create a successful hybrid schedule include the following:

- Build regularity into your schedule. The repetition and predictability will be less taxing on your mental health than an erratic schedule. It will also make you a reliable coworker. Your baristas will be happy. They can count on you every Monday, Wednesday, and Friday.
- Reflect on your personal and work commitments and generate a schedule that you can stick to. To the degree that things change, plan at least a week or so in advance.
- Try different options. You'll save mental energy if you have a regular schedule. Communicate your schedule to others to stop them from reaching out to you at all times of the day.

LACK OF BOUNDARIES

A lack of boundaries between work and home is exhausting. Our home is our office. Work bleeds into everything. We've moved from the myth of separate worlds to acknowledging we don't have any separation between our work life and our home life. This lack of boundaries peaked in 2020 when people were working from home full-time. Oxford Languages announced a new word: *blursday*—"Difficulty in determining what day of the week it is." The essence of *blursday* is the lack of boundaries in our lives—not just between work and home but within each day. Without boundaries, our stress levels go up.

Action steps to build boundaries in your life include the following:

- Build microtransitions into your day. Every day. Microtransitions are small tasks, rituals, and activities that break up a day. Going into the office includes lots of microtransitions: getting dressed in work clothes, leaving the house; commuting; buying coffee. When working from home, create similar microtransitions: get dressed in work clothes; go out to get coffee; meet your spouse, child, or housemate for breakfast at a certain time.
- Build microtransitions with others. They can be fun, productive, meditative, or social. Listen to music at a certain time. Read a book with your child. At dinner, ask your partner what was special about the day. Fun Fridays. Quiet Sundays.
- Set start and stop times for your workday. At the start time, begin your workday with a ritual such as bringing your coffee to your desk; saying to yourself, "Time to go to work"; opening your computer; or checking the day's schedule. At the stop time, have a stop ritual such as reviewing your calendar for the next workday; finishing one last email; powering down your computer; tidying up your desk; saying to yourself, "Time to go home"; or walking away from your desk.

Be conscious of using rituals like these as your commute to and from work. Many people say an advantage of working from home is not having to commute. But commutes help create boundaries and therefore potentially decrease stress.

ZOOM FATIGUE

Well, Oxford didn't mention *Zoom fatigue*, but the term did make it into Wikipedia. As you would expect, it's the burned-out feeling that results from using and overusing virtual platforms of communication.

The fatigue is due to several factors. When we're using platforms like these, there's an excessive amount of staring. No one breaks eye contact as we do in person to decrease the intensity of a connection. What is the size of your face on the screen? It is based on how close you are to your camera, but it's probably less than eighteen inches, which is a typical distance for intimate relationships. Imagine how it feels to be standing in front of someone at the office but as close as you are to your camera. The average amount of personal space for Americans who are close or socially connected is eighteen to twenty-four inches, meaning most Americans are comfortable with an arm's length of personal space. Alas, you're in intense relationships all day long.

When in live meetings, participants tend to glance around the room, make eye contact with one person at a time, or look down at their phone or computer. It breaks up the intensity and gives them a break from being on. Imagine sitting in a meeting room and everyone staring at you regardless of whether you are speaking or not. On Zoom, as everyone is staring at the same camera, it feels like everyone is staring at you. It's cognitive overload as you take in everyone's scrutiny.

Your range of motion during a virtual meeting is limited. There is overemphasis on your head, and other than your arms a little bit, you don't move. You can't move your legs because if you do, it's annoying to others. Have you ever been in a Zoom meeting with someone who is at a standing desk and moving back and forth or side to side? The only good news is that you can wear pajama bottoms and no one will know.

Most people speak loudly on Zoom meetings. Yet imagine how exhausting it would be to speak loudly all day at the office.

Sensory overload is taxing. Our screens are filled with people all sitting in different rooms. Unlike conference rooms with white walls, people's rooms are filled with books, pictures, laundry, beds, kitchen tables, all kinds of things. Filtering out all the extra things takes mental energy. Not to mention ignoring the cute dog in the background or, worse, that barking dog down the hall.

Action steps to minimize zoom fatigue include the following:
Move your camera so you're sitting twelve to eighteen inches from it. Ask your teammates to do the same.

- Allow time for pre-meetings. This can accomplish the same thing that would happen when you were in the office and had to walk from meeting to meeting. Office meetings frequently start five to ten minutes late due to this transition time. Pre-meetings are transition times.
- Build in breaks, including a stretch break.

- Shorten meetings by five to ten minutes or try to schedule shorter meetings.
- Get a standing desk and alternate standing and sitting.
- Use headphones and work at lowering your voice.
- Call if that's an option, because people don't yell on the phone and you can walk around.
- Have everyone blur his or her background or use a common background to decrease cognitive load.
- Take video breaks. Have everyone turn off the video function for a certain amount of time during the meeting.
- Hide self-view to decrease the feeling of constantly being scrutinized.
- Conduct a meeting inventory ahead of time to see if the meeting is really needed.

LIMITED CONNECTIONS

Flexible work involves people coming and going at different times. And connections other than in person aren't as fluid and conducive to building interpersonal glue. The quality and quantity of your relationships is a powerful component of your work world. Interpersonal glue breeds support. Strained relationships cause stress—especially with one's boss. Remember: "People join companies and leave managers." A Gallop study found one of two employees leave a job sometime in their career to get away from a bad manager and improve their general well-being.[2] You can't assume you'll bump into someone in the hall so that's one more thing to think about. Do you want to go out to dinner with someone after work? First you have to ask yourself if they're in the office Tuesday, Wednesday, or Thursday. Maybe you want to have a live brainstorming session with them one morning. But what time do they come in?

Action Stepsto reduce the randomness of team interaction include the following:

- Create a team calendar in order for everyone to see who is working where and when.

- Allow time in your calendar every in-office day to make a connection with someone.
- Build time into meetings to connect on a personal level.
- Initiate out-of-work fun activities with coworkers.
- Randomly call someone who is working remotely to say hi.
- Include money in the budget for fun and food (*team building* looks better on the ledger).
- Schedule lunch with coworkers you can lean on.

BURNOUT

As noted in chapter 11, burnout is a mental health issue, a psychological syndrome that results from job stress, which can result from spillover between work and personal life as well as many other things.

How do you know if you're burned out? Ask yourself:

1. Am I experiencing any of the causes of burnout?
2. Do I have any of the symptoms of burnout?

Causes of Burnout

1. Role clarity: My responsibilities are not clear, or I don't have control over my work.
2. Workload: I have too much work or unreasonable deadlines.
3. Valued contributor: My skills and talents aren't used at work.
4. Praise and recognition: I don't receive recognition or rewards for good performance.
5. Poor communication: Communication is limited, or it is difficult to express opinions or feelings.
6. Weak team: I don't have a strong team or enough resources.
7. Difficult boss: My boss is difficult or unavailable.
8. Unsupportive coworkers: I feel alone and unsupported.
9. Unfair treatment: I've experienced bias, missed opportunities, or unfair compensation.
10. Work–life balance: Work is spilling over and interfering with my personal life.

Mental Health Symptoms of Burnout

1. Mentally exhausted
2. Cynical toward or critical of work
3. Irritable or inpatient with others
4. Distracted or unable to concentrate
5. Lacking job satisfaction
6. Detached from others or feel alone
7. Less productive
8. Cynical or not aligned with company
9. Depressed
10. Anxious

Physical Symptoms of Burnout

1. Physically exhausted and tired
2. Sleeping—more or less than usual
3. Drinking or drug use—more than usual
4. Eating—more or less than usual or eating more junk food
5. Body-, stomach-, or headaches

Managing burnout includes managing both your work and personal world.

Action Steps to avert burnout include the following:

- Be proactive, define your own role, and discuss with your stakeholders.
- Delegate more and seek additional resources.
- Set limits or say no when appropriate.
- Set reasonable goals.
- Be creative and offer to contribute in new ways.
- Remember to value yourself.
- Ask for feedback, a pay increase, or a promotion.
- Flex to other people's communication styles.
- Remember that developing your team is your job. Change priorities to allow time for development.

- Ask your boss how he or she likes to work together. Assert your preferences and adapt as necessary.
- Initiate social contact with others.
- Ask for help and support your coworkers.
- Seek assistance from a manager or human resources.
- Build boundaries, rituals, and transitions into your life.

START WITH YOU

Your general well-being is enhanced by a diversity of wellness strategies and coping mechanisms. More is better. For example, exercise has consistently been shown to be an essential part of healthy living and managing burnout. However, during a stressful meeting, you can't say, "Please hold on for about an hour. I need to hit the gym." There are other things we do to cope that really aren't helpful. Table 15.1 lists ways of coping that can be helpful or not so helpful.

Keep in mind there are lots of ways to cope with burnout. Build your personal toolbox. The more you have in your toolbox, the better. As we have said before, pick one new thing to do. After that becomes a habit, add a second. But remember, one comes before two.

Table 15.1

	Helpful	*Not Helpful*
Mental Health	Breathe or meditate. Talk with friends and coworkers. Maintain a positive, optimistic attitude. Seek professional help when needed.	Be always on the go. Keep thoughts and feeling inside. Have a negative, pessimistic view of the world. Keep an inventory of your faults.
Work–Life Balance	Create work-life boundaries. Set limits or say no when appropriate. Plan and maintain a weekly schedule. Play. Do something fun.	Don't create work–life boundaries. Always say yes even when you're busy. Take each day as it comes. Assume others can read your mind.
Physical Health	Exercise, stretch, or take a walk. Eat healthy. Listen to your body. Seek medical help when needed.	Don't make time for exercise. Snack on junk food or drink coffee all day long. Ignore physical aches and pains. Drink too much or abuse substances.
Interpersonal Glue	Support teammates. Socialize with coworkers. Communicate openly and honestly. Connect and socialize with friends and family.	Work independently. Spend too much time at your computer. Withhold information and ignore others. Spend all your personal time alone.
Productivity	Manage your time and plan a daily schedule. Take breaks. Seek excellence and set reasonable goals. Problem solve or brainstorm with others.	Procrastinate and constantly work under pressure. Work until exhaustion sets in. Seek perfection and set unrealistic goals. Stay committed to past ways of working.

Section IV

GUARDRAILS FOR SUCCESS IN HYBRID WORK

The guardrails address important issues that organizations must be cognizant of as they take steps to institute greater flexibility as to where and when work is performed. They highlight how increased flexibility can unleash opportunities to improve employee engagement and support efforts to enhance diversity, equity, and inclusion. Yet, as organizations embrace greater flexibility, new issues will arise. Key among these issues is potential bias against employees who work remotely or take advantage of hybrid opportunities. The guardrails explore how bias can undermine efforts to engage all employees and present strategies for proactively addressing potential bias. The chapters that follow highlight critical compliance issues that will emerge in organizations as their workforce expands geographically and offer a roadmap to avoid compliance mishaps.

Chapter Sixteen

Advancing Environmental, Social, Governance (ESG) and Diversity, Equity, and Inclusion (DEI) Goals

In this chapter we point out the intersection between supporting flexible work arrangements and an organization's environmental, social, governance (ESG) and diversity, equity, and inclusion (DEI) goals. Our premise is that a strong commitment to flexible work, including but not limited to embracing hybrid work arrangements, supports ESG and DEI goals. There is a meaningful overlap between these concepts that should be fully mined. Look at your organizations' transition to a hybrid work structure and flexible work in general as one component of an ESG or DEI program. As we will discuss, the opportunities for hybrid work arrangements to improve ESG and DEI performance are meaningful and many.

High on every business leader's list of priorities is enhancing their organization's ESG performance. The focus on ESG reached new heights in the 2020s. We start our discussion with definitions.

- *environmental*: issues focused on climate risk, carbon emissions, energy efficiency, use of natural resources, biodiversity
- *social*: issues focused on human capital including diversity, equity, and inclusion; labor regulations; worker safety; human rights; and community engagement
- *governance*: issues focused on board diversity, corruption and bribery, business ethics, compensation policies, and general risk tolerance

For businesses, stakeholders are increasingly asking leaders to define their enterprise's ESG goals, articulate a program to effectuate these goals, and finally, to demonstrate how these goals have been met. While investors served as the original stakeholders in ESG performance, they are not the only stakeholders whose voice business leaders must now listen to. On the contrary, boards of directors, consumers, and employees are playing an outsize role in demanding to know what each enterprise's intentions are to favorably impact the environment, support social causes, and ensure transparency and ethical business dealings. Thus, for leaders of even small businesses, ESG performance can enhance an organization's reputation and provide a vehicle for the organization to distinguish itself from its competitors. There is no question that applicants and employees care deeply about their organization's mission and place in the larger world order. Well-defined ESG goals, a true program to achieve those goals, and tangible outcomes will enable an organization to establish best-in-class credentials, furthering the organization's ability to attract and retain talent.

With a focus on the intersection of hybrid work and ESG, think of the *E* in *environmental impact* as a starting point. Much has been reported about the impact that the 2020 lockdowns had on energy use. There was a record drop in global carbon emissions in 2020 as a result of a reduction in economic activity as well as a shift to more remote work. The way in which organizations conducted business changed dramatically during the shutdown, and many changes endured. The reduction of miles commuted translated into less fossil fuel use leading to improved air quality and potentially a reduction in the carbon footprint associated with work. Likewise paper consumption was reduced as employees working from home were less likely to print documents and more likely to use digital document management systems and e-signature platforms. Use of single-use plasticware—cups, cutlery, and the like, purchased for office use—also fell significantly during the shutdowns.

On the other side of the equation, streaming—particularly the use of video—increased, and streaming requires significant electricity usage that should be considered in evaluating the net impact of any increase in remote work arrangements.[1] What this means is moving to a remote-first approach does not necessarily translate to a significant reduction in energy use. It's more complicated. During the 2020 shutdowns and thereafter, we learned that while offices used less power because they were not occupied or not fully occupied, power consumption by individuals at home rose. Employees working at home needed to be online, to heat and cool their homes, to charge their devices. An article in the *Guardian* presented a surprising bottom line on energy use.

In some parts of the country during lockdown, average home electricity consumption rose more than 20 percent on weekdays, according to the International Energy Agency. IEA's analysis suggests workers who use public transport or drive less than four miles each way could actually increase their total emissions by working from home.[2]

On the whole, however, working away from an office can have a positive impact on climate change. Companies should assess the changes that they can identify as a result of embracing hybrid work and communicate to stakeholders the positive impact of these changes.

A true assessment of the impact of an organization's flexible approach to work on the environment requires analysis of many different practices. Simply allowing employees to work from home some of the time while maintaining the same real estate footprint is not likely to achieve great reductions in that organization's carbon footprint. Likewise, reverting to the pre-pandemic practice of jumping on a plane to go to a luncheon or single-purpose meeting will also not contribute to reduced carbon emissions. According to a report by the Global Business Travel Association based on a survey of 220 corporate travel managers in the United States and Canada in April 2021, close to half the companies surveyed aspired to focus on the social and environmental impact of business travel post-pandemic. The surveyed companies indicated that they expected to do so by restricting travel. Yet most of the surveyed companies did not have a formal business travel sustainability program. The absence of such a program would lead one to wonder how these goals would be affected.

A paradox emerges: Employers see the opportunity to cast a wider net geographically for talent, but as this distributed workforce emerges so does the need to create opportunities for in-person meetings so team members can connect. The need to engender interpersonal glue is a fundamental one for organizations. While the surveyed companies claimed to want their travel programs to reflect a more socially and environmentally conscious approach, in the absence of an articulated and published program, their efforts to reduce travel and its accompanying carbon footprint might be haphazard and ineffective.

Organizations that are serious about making a change in workplace practices to create a net positive environmental impact must prioritize the goal of carbon footprint reduction and commit to such a goal with meaningful and identifiable actions. Eric Friedrichsen, CEO of Emburse, argues that corporations that want to do more than just tick a box must commit to change travel practices and communicate those goals to employees.[3] When leaders think twice before flying to attend a meeting and demonstrate these actions to others in their organization, they can change how employees view travel. Requiring employees to articulate the business proposition justifying a trip is one way to raise consciousness about the environmental impact of travel. Changing corporate culture with behavioral shifts will have a more meaningful impact if leaders explain that the reason for reining in business travel is not simply to reap short-term financial savings but to support the long-term goal of enhanced sustainability.

Because hybrid and remote work arrangements do not necessarily ensure a net positive impact on the environment, organizations with a commitment to sustainability should also look to reducing the carbon footprint resulting from their real estate holdings. This means shrinking the size and number of offices and transitioning to greener workplaces. The most obvious opportunity for a positive environmental impact may be created when an enterprise reduces its office space requirements. Hybrid work schedules can provide an opportunity for office sizes to shrink when schedules are developed with this goal in mind.

Earlier we introduced the concept of hoteling, which is the practice of sharing workspaces. Companies can move toward hoteling wherein every employee does not have his or her own personal workstation but instead works at any workspace. Booking technology is often used by companies using the hoteling concept so that an employee books a location on a daily basis. Organizations might reduce their real estate footprint significantly this way depending on how split shifts are organized.

Hybrid arrangements also offer enterprises the opportunity to maintain smaller offices in more locations, which also can lead to smaller real estate footprints. In its *Global Outlook 2030*, CBRE, a commercial real estate firm, predicts nearly all employees will one day be mobile and require a network of locations to be productive and engaged.[4] As organizations change their real estate needs, these changes will enhance opportunities to pursue space in greener buildings.

Initially it was the COVID-19 pandemic that drove enterprises to right-size their commercial real estate portfolios, but with a long-term commitment to hybrid work models, enterprises have a remarkable opportunity to create long-term sustainability performance both within the office environment and at home while supporting the transition to a low-carbon economy. When companies can count on a portion of their workforce working remotely on a regular basis, these hybrid arrangements should result in fewer employees in the workplace daily. Organizations should pursue opportunities to reduce the number of workstations and shrink the square footage of their total office space. This will have a positive impact on net emissions. And where opportunities exist to move to green buildings that take advantage of energy efficiencies, these moves can play an outsize role in demonstrating an organization's commitment to sustainability.

SET GOALS FOR
IMPROVED SUSTAINABILITY

Building an infrastructure that fosters a culture of sustainability requires the commitment of your organization's leaders. The first step is educating leaders as to the importance of this long-term commitment. The second step is advising employees that leadership has made such a commitment and that all employees have a role to play in reaching sustainability goals. Here are our suggestions:

- Include environmental sustainability as part of your organization's mission statement.
- Promote awareness of environmental concerns.
- Communicate steps your organization has and will take to support sustainability. This may include reducing office space, moving to hoteling arrangements, identifying opportunities to move to green real estate, reducing business travel, and revamping office recycling protocols.
- Communicate to employees that their individual decisions and behavior can favorably impact the environment; for example, using

public transportation, carpooling, or walking or biking to work when possible; limiting business travel to circumstances when presence is truly important to a business goal; and considering waste by limiting the use of paper and disposables.

- Create policies supporting remote and hybrid work.
- Support other businesses that share this mission.

Hybrid work arrangements can also support your enterprise's commitment to social responsibility, the *S* in *ESG*. Organizations should view the hybrid work model as a gateway to greater diversity, supporting parents and caregivers while supporting employees' desire to engage with their communities. Employee surveys support this notion. *Future Forum*'s October 2021 survey showed that a diverse group of employees overwhelmingly want flexible work programs.

- 87 percent of Asian respondents
- 81 percent of Black respondents
- 78 percent of Hispanic respondents
- 75 percent of white respondents[5]

These findings are not surprising. An argument can be made that the presence of flexible work arrangements or a flexible schedule are concrete evidence that an organization is committed to inclusiveness.

The social aspects of ESG include establishing and committing to adherence to policies providing for equal employment opportunity and the prevention of harassment in the workplace. The willingness of an organization to embrace flexible work patterns goes hand in hand with DEI initiatives. Those organizations whose policies encourage employees to seek alternative arrangements are viewed as supporting inclusiveness.

Total rewards programs focusing on flexible work arrangements play an important role in messaging your organization's social commitment. Programs like those listed below message to employees and outside stakeholders that your enterprise is serious about its commitment to supporting inclusiveness and creating a more equitable workplace.

- employee training programs that focus on skills building, collaboration, and individual development
- opportunities for leaves of absences to address family commitments, education, and healthcare challenges

- programs providing for financial support for educational pursuits
- flexible work hours to allow ample time to address child and dependent care obligations
- sabbaticals to advert burnout or enable the pursuit of a personal opportunity
- meaningful mentorship programs
- well-defined opportunities for advancement with coaching opportunities
- emphasis on recruiting diverse talent and a meaningful DEI program with defined goals and a review of achievement
- a focus on development of a pipeline of future leaders including a commitment to succession planning

While the programs listed above could be managed by human capital professionals, an organization that really excels in meeting its social goals will engage all its leaders in a commitment to the successful outcomes of these programs. Human capital professionals alone cannot carry an organization's obligation to buy into and support these goals. Much has been said about the importance of empathy in developing human capital. Leaders must recognize that job arrangements and changes to those arrangements can have a significant impact on an employee's ability to manage his or her household.

How can a hybrid approach support these programs and goals? Hybrid work provides an opportunity for flexibility that could not be achieved when all employees were expected to report to a physical office five days each week. Whether the hybrid protocol permits employees to adjust their work hours or days or reduce the lost time that would typically be spent commuting, enlightened leaders can find ways to support their colleagues in a hybrid work environment. We've discussed how cultivating talent can incorporate new techniques such as by casting a wider geographic net when remote work is permitted. Likewise, when remote work is part of a hybrid work environment, that wider net can include more diverse candidates who might not be available to work for the enterprise if they had to report to a single location every day. Likewise, allyship and skills-building programs that are based on remote training opportunities can also widen the path for employees who might not be able to participate if they were required to be present in an office all of the time.

As the dust began to settle following the migration to remote work in 2020, we began to see reports showing that Black workers in particular favored working remotely. By the fall of 2021, news outlets were reporting that Black Americans prefer working remotely because of the emotional toll of working in workplaces dominated by whites. According to a CBS news report, a substantial number of Black employees preferred working away from the office because remote work allows them to avoid microaggression.[6] *HuffPost* published a similar story and reported that Black employees felt a stronger sense of inclusion when not working in an office environment.[7]

We would like to hope that organizations reviewing these reports think carefully about why the workplace experience is markedly poorer for Black employees and not pursue remote work options as a way to reduce racism in the workplace. An effective DEI program should address intentional and unintentional bias and the impact that microaggressions have on colleagues.

Finally, an enterprise's social contract also includes community engagement. Not long ago, community engagement was typically limited to the community in which the enterprise's corporate office was located. Employers demonstrated community engagement with an occasional community-based project—a volunteer day when employees cleaned a local park, painted a school, or worked in a soup kitchen for example. The hybrid model opens the enterprise up to a broader array of engagement opportunities including longer-term and more meaningful engagement activities. As the in-person model of community service becomes only one method, opportunities for community engagement can extend to online connections. Service work supporting schools, not-for-profit organizations, and community service organizations is increasingly performed virtually. Coaching and mentoring students and new entrants to the workplace are now performed remotely, permitting greater employee participation. Community engagement projects that include greater numbers of employees will have a stronger impact on your organization's goals. Organizations with a serious commitment to the community will want to approach the concept of community service in a new way and broaden their horizon to include projects that will engage the entire workforce regardless of where employees reside.

ASSESS WHETHER TOTAL REWARDS PROGRAMS ARE IN LINE WITH SOCIAL GOALS

Supporting the social goals of a workforce requires both a policy infrastructure that fosters a culture of inclusion and engagement and the commitment of the organization's leaders. Assessing whether an organization supports social engagement in a meaningful way is to review the organization's policies and total rewards programs. Perhaps the newest trend is offering fertility benefits to all employees including LGBTQ+ and single prospective parents. Such benefits, which may include the cost of in vitro fertilization (IVF), egg freezing and harvesting services, and adoption, is a positive way to create a more inclusive workplace. Fertility benefits may be highly valued by talent no matter their gender identity or relationship status.

Creating benefits that encourage allyship, support leave policies, and address burnout are important elements of the social contract between organizations and their employees. But organizations need to evaluate whether these policies are working. Are employees using the leave and benefit packages? Or is there an underlying stigma against taking advantage of the offerings because to do so demonstrates less than 100 percent commitment to the workplace? Here are our suggestions for conducting such an assessment.

1. Identify policies that support families.

   a. childcare leave for birth, adoption, and foster care placement for both men and women
   b. family care leave for both men and women
   c. family forming benefits (leave or financial support for IVF treatments and financial assistance for adoptions)
   d. leave time to attend to ill family members
   e. leave time to attend to school matters

2. Identify programs that allow for flexible or reduced work obligations to address employees' need to devote time to their family.

   a. flexibility to work remotely or on a hybrid schedule
   b. flexibility to shift work hours to accommodate personal obligations

   c. ability to transition to a part-time work schedule on a permanent or short-term basis

3. Identify steps to evaluate the effectiveness of such policies.

   a. How well are the policies communicated? Is a broader and more-inclusive communications program necessary?
   b. Are leaders utilizing the policies?
   c. What is the utilization rate of the benefits? Are the benefits increasingly popular or is their use on the decline?
   d. Are leaders supporting employees who use the policies?
   e. What are employee retention rates for those employees who use the policies?
   f. Do exit interviews indicate that employees do not feel supported when they use the policies or are concerned about retaliation if they use the policies?
   g. Are employees progressing in the organization after taking advantage of these benefits?

Governance in the context of ESG is essentially about how an organization is managed by those who were once relegated to the top floor executive offices but in a hybrid work scenario will hopefully be more approachable. How transparent is the work of the executive management and the board of directors? First and perhaps foremost, do the board members and company executives represent a diverse range of voices and experiences? Is decision making transparent? Are key decisions shared by employees and other stakeholders?

ENSURE THAT DIFFERENT VOICES IMPACT THE FLEXIBLE WORK APPROACH

In earlier chapters we made suggestions regarding the formulation of the flexible work policy. We started our discussion with the assembly of the team that would serve as the task force to develop the policy. We urged leaders to ensure that the task force included many voices, not just those of the C-suite. Input from varied voices will contribute to better decision making in the long run.

Chapter Seventeen

Supporting DEI and Addressing Proximity Bias

Felice heard from a venture capital leader who runs funds that exclusively support female entrepreneurs about the impact hybrid work arrangements could have on women in the workplace. This leader—a woman who works hard to support other female leaders—expressed concern that the increased flexibility employees have in choosing where to work would result in setbacks for women, in particular mothers with caregiving responsibilities. Here's how this leader saw the problem playing out. Organizations would permit and perhaps even encourage employees to work from home on an exclusive or optional basis, and those most likely to elect the remote option would be women with children or other caregiving responsibilities. While she acknowledged the hybrid work option was an excellent way to support and retain women, this leader was concerned that those employees reporting to the office on a regular basis would be employees with fewer family obligations: traditionally, men. The venture capital leader noted that the long-term impact of women working away from the office would be women out of sight, out of mind, meaning that women would not be around to be in the right place at the right time and would not be viewed as available for choice assignments or to be pulled into impromptu meetings, and most critically, would not be viewed as committed because they chose to work from home.

This was not the musings of one tuned-in entrepreneur. The concept of remote employees as out of sight, out of mind is well accepted. A report issued by the Society for Human Resources Management (SHRM) in June called this concern "acute."[1] SHRM's report predicted that when given the choice, women will choose to work remotely to better manage family obligations and will thus be relegated to second-tier status in the workplace. A SHRM survey of 817 supervisors conducted in July 2021 found the folllowing of responding supervisors:

- 67 percent admitted to considering remote workers more easily replaceable than on-site workers at their organization
- 62 percent believed full-time remote work was detrimental to employees' career objectives
- 72 percent said they would prefer all their subordinates to be working in the office
- 42 percent said they sometimes forgot about remote workers when assigning tasks
- 67 percent said they spent more time supervising remote workers than on-site workers[2]

What do these data points show us? The possibility of proximity bias is real. Essentially, the survey demonstrates that these supervisors are biased. They don't like the fact that they must oversee a distributed workforce, and they do not favor their remote team members.

We urge organizations to address the real threat of proximity bias. Proximity bias is the mistaken assumption that those employees who are physically present are more engaged and more productive. It is a type of cognitive bias, meaning it is a preconceived view or opinion that gets in the way of decision making. Proximity bias is not new; it's been around for a long time. Think about the old days when those sitting closer to the boss's office (or hanging around the boss's office) were more likely to be invited to lunch or to attend an important meeting. That's proximity bias. Proximity bias can impact the development and retention of talent in organizations that provide hybrid work alternatives or allow some employees to work remotely. Proximity bias is simply on-site favoritism, because employees who work on-site get more advancement opportunities than employees who don't. If more women and people of color choose hybrid schedules and more men and white people choose to be fully on-site, the results are predictable. On-site favoritism will predictably happen unless organizations take steps to ensure it doesn't. Bias against employees who are working remotely or on a hybrid schedule will undo any organization's efforts to support equity and inclusion (see chapter 16).

Proximity bias is real. At a *Wall Street Journal* event, Sandeep Mathrani, the CEO of WeWork, opined that employees who are the least engaged want to work remotely.[3] The *Wall Street Journal* further reported that Mathrani said, "People are happier when they come to work." Leaders who articulate these positions and yet offer hybrid or remote options are telegraphing to their employees: We are offering the remote and hybrid options so we can check that box, but we really want you in the office. A year later, the *New York Times* reported on this topic, focusing on the impact of remote work on new employees, who need to forge a place in an organization and learn from more experienced colleagues.[4] The article highlighted the efforts of some organizations to teach leaders to recognize proximity bias and the work necessary to address it.

A *Wall Street Journal* article titled "How to Gameplan Your Office Days: An Overachiever's Guide to Hybrid Work" is actually a how-to guide for workers who want to make the most of proximity bias by monopolizing access to leaders.[5] The article acknowledges that face time with leaders will be in short supply when leaders and their teams are present in an office only some of the time. The author recommends that employees figure out when leaders will be in their offices and show up on those days. For added impact, a team member should report to work on the days the boss is in, but most employees are not—for example Fridays, a day when most employees will want to be working from home. Better yet, the author suggests, show up every day for maximum impact! So, there you have it: a guide to making the most of a leader's bias by being the most present!

Organizations must pay attention to proximity bias as they manage the hybrid workplace. During the pandemic more than two million women reportedly left the workforce because of their inability to navigate the challenges presented when school and daycare programs closed. If women are to be lured back to the workplace, organizations must keep their eye on the importance of creating opportunities providing women (and all employees for that matter) with the ability to create a work–life balance. Otherwise, the loss of talent in the workplace will be magnified. The *Women in the Workplace 2020* report issued by McKinsey & Company and LeanIn.Org focuses on what the authors refer to as the "state of the pipeline" and warns that as a result of the drop-out rate of women in the workforce in 2020, women will be held back from future opportunities.[6] The report projected a bleak picture of the future where the pool of candidates for consideration for executive positions would reflect decreasing numbers of women and even lower numbers of women of color if the loss of talent that resulted from the pandemic is not reversed.

Proximity bias can be interrupted but only if leaders take affirmative steps. Intentionality is required. First, organizations should not promote the misguided belief that employees who work remotely are less committed and less available. If an organization chooses to embrace hybrid options, then employees who avail themselves of these arrangements should not be penalized. Leaders must be reminded that when an organization endorses flexibility, leaders must proactively ensure that those employees working remotely are given equal access to opportunities even if they are out of sight.

Making certain that remote workers are not forgotten takes work. Leaders must learn to interrupt their behavior—meaning that leaders must recognize when proximity bias exists. How can leaders be more aware so they can stop biased thinking and decision making? The first step is training. Teaching leaders to recognize bias—including proximity bias—is the first step forward. The second step is to create protocols that will actually force leaders to interact with team members consistently. Casual meetings must be replaced with more scheduled interactions. While some leaders might find this directive burdensome, intentionality is required when directing a hybrid team.

COMBAT PROXIMITY BIAS

Highest on the list of steps an organization should take to battle proximity bias is training. Anti-bias training is a critical component of a DEI program. Proximity bias is just one of the cognitive biases that need to be identified and interrupted as a first step in promoting inclusiveness in a workplace. Training is the first step to self-awareness. How can an organization's leaders tout their forward-thinking hybrid options when those who avail themselves of the flexibility to work from home never get a chance to get ahead? That's the likely outcome unless leaders truly buy in to the advantages of hybrid arrangements.

Here is a review of our key suggestions:

- Provide anti-bias training for leaders. Such training will include proximity bias as well as other forms of cognitive bias that can get in the way of ensuring engagement and opportunity for all emploees. Enlighten leaders as to how micro-aggression impacts workers ("You're never in the office when I need you!").
- Evaluate leaders based on their ability to develop their entire team. Some organizations focus leaders on the importance of developing talent from the moment an individual is responsible for a team. When leaders are responsible for leading a team that is distributed—meaning some work on-site, some work remotely, and yet others have a hybrid schedule—not only do leaders need training to learn how to be successful, they need to be rewarded when they develop talent.
- Survey employees working remotely or on hybrid schedules. Learn about their experiences. Do remote employees perceive that they are treated as equals and if not, what are the issues? Consider creating a focus group made up of remote employees and leaders to discuss what steps could be taken to improve integration of remote staff and ensure equal access to opportunities for remote staff. Undertake the same assessment of the hybrid workforce.
- Analyze data regarding promotions. Are remote employees successful in working their way up the corporate ladder? If not, why not?
- Analyze exit interview data. What are the issues raised by remote employees and how do these issues compare with those identified with employees who are not remote?
- Teach leaders how to manage teams that include remote, hybrid, and on-site workers. Leading teams when employees work in varying places requires a new skill set.
- Identify a human resources leader whose responsibilities specifically include ensuring that remote employees are engaged and fully integrated in the workplace.

AVOID PROXIMITY BIAS

We urge leaders who lead teams that include remote employees, employees on hybrid schedules, or on-site employees not to rely on their good intentions to ensure that they do not favor these who are on-site. Rather it is essential to take affirmative steps to ensure all team members enjoy equal access to leaders and opportunity. Many of the action items we discussed in section II will also help interrupt proximity bias. Here is a review of our key suggestions:

- Schedule weekly supervision sessions with each team member. If once a week is unrealistic, every other week will do. Meetings can be for as short as fifteen minutes if this is a check-in without an agenda. Regularly calendared meetings ensure that every team member has access to the leader and does not have to rely on an impromptu meeting at the coffee machine.
- Schedule a longer period of time for each team member to regularly speak with you about their goals. Talking about professional growth and goals should not take place exclusively during the annual performance evaluation. Employees should be provided with other opportunities to speak with their leader about where they can hope to go next in the organization and how to get there. With some employees this will happen organically, with other employees the time must be scheduled. For employees working remotely these sessions will replace lunch or afterwork get-togethers where these topics would be approached in an informal manner. The only way that remote employees will have the same opportunities as employees working on-site is to be affirmative!
- Keep a calendar of when team members join you for informal lunch, coffee, or an afterwork drink. Identify who was invited, and if some team members are never included, make a date with them.
- Keep a list of key projects and who was assigned. Particularly where there are projects that are likely to give team members visibility within your organization, keep track of which team members were given the opportunity so that assignments can be disbursed fairly. The list will enable you to be sure that all team members have comparable opportunities.
- Keep a list of occasions when you've brought a team member to a high-level meeting or customer pitch. Again, the list will permit you to track who has been provided with opportunities and who is next up. The only way to be sure that opportunities are distributed fairly among all employees is to keep a record. Recollections are skewed.
- Recognize your personal bias and take steps to interrupt it. Managing teams of both remote and on-site employees is tough and complicated

by our natural inclination to do what's easiest, which may be to follow our affinity bias and connect more readily with employees whom we share commonality with (e.g., women may feel more comfortable dealing with women). Availability bias can also come into play when what's top of mind takes over, which is why the out-of-sight-out-of-mind problem is so real. Organizations are increasingly recognizing that bias steps in the way of diversity and inclusion efforts, and for this reason training to avoid bias is a necessary part of ensuring inclusion. The need for this training is even more compelling when leaders are challenged to manage two separate cohorts—remote employees and on-site employees.

Chapter Eighteen

Avoiding Pay Equity and Discrimination Claims

Money is important.

As employers embrace flexible work arrangements, new questions about compensation practices will arise. Leaders are asking new questions about compensation management as they embrace flexible work arrangements.

- Should employees be paid differently depending on where they fall in the hybrid work spectrum?
- Should remote workers be paid less for the privilege of working from home and not commuting?
- Should employees who agree to commute to an office every day be rewarded for doing so?
- What are the legal ramifications of a policy where pay is based on where employees work?

While there is no single answer to these questions, companies must balance pay equity obligations alongside fairness concerns, staff morale, and recruitment goals. And most important, companies must ensure that their compensation practices do not result in inequity.

UNDERSTANDING PAY EQUITY

Pay equity is a movement toward erasing the gaps in compensation that may be due to gender or race discrimination. Ensuring that compensation is managed in an equitable way also is a critical component of a successful DEI program.

The disparity in pay between men and women and between white employees and employees of color has long existed. These gaps have hardly closed in the decades since they were first published. According to the US Census Bureau, which has been monitoring the gap in wages between men and women since 1960, we've seen very limited movement in close to sixty years. In 1960 women earned about 61 percent of wages earned by men on average. By 2018 that number had crept up to 81.6 percent. By 2020 women earned only 84 percent of what their male counterparts earned.[1] Some may see this as an improvement, but others view the lingering impact of wage discrimination as grossly unfair. The racial pay gap in the United States also has hardly improved. A report issued by the Society for Human Resources Management in June 2020 reported that Black men earn only $0.87 for every dollar a white male earns. Hispanic men fair only slightly better at $0.91 for every dollar.

The focus of the pay equity movement is to erase differences in pay that cannot be explained by legitimate reasons and exist due to discriminatory reasons. In the past few years, the pay equity movement has seen a robust resurgence with more and more companies taking affirmative steps to ensure that their compensation schemes are fair and unbiased. Another survey conducted by the Society for Human Resources Management found that 58 percent of organizations surveyed voluntarily conducted a pay equity review to identify possible pay differences between employees performing similar work. The report further found that as a result of these reviews, 83 percent of these organization adjusted pay.[2]

A discussion of pay equity is necessary when considering flexible work arrangements: If an organization offers different work arrangements with different pay levels, the organization must be cognizant of the possibility that in doing so, pay equity issues may be exacerbated. Likewise, employees should proceed with caution when faced with the choice of a higher or lower wage depending on *where* work is performed.

Are employers who choose to make compensation decisions based on location or remote status creating a risk that their compensation schemes will be deemed discriminatory? What approach should an employer seeking best-in-class status take to setting pay in a hybrid work setting? We begin our discussion with a review of the legal backdrop relating to discrimination based on pay.

LEGAL UNDERPINNINGS OF PAY EQUITY

A number of federal statutes address aspects of pay equity. The federal Equal Pay Act (EPA) passed in 1963 prohibits employers from engaging in sex-based pay discrimination. Title VII of the Civil Rights Act of 1964 and Executive Order 11246 also prohibit pay discrimination based on race and other protected characteristics. The National Labor Relations Act (NLRA) also protects employees' right to discuss information about wages. The Office of Federal Contract Compliance Programs (OFCCP) enforces the nondiscrimination provisions of Executive Order 11246 including the ban on compensation discrimination. These federal laws apply to all but the smallest employers in the United States.

The EPA established the principle of equal pay for equal work and forbids sex-based pay discrimination. The EPA provides employers with affirmative defenses that employers can rely on to explain why men and women are not compensated the same for equal work performed under similar working experiences. One of these defenses is that the employer can implement wage differentials "based on any factor other than sex." It is this defense that employers turn to when setting wages based on geolocation, or years of experience, or tenure with a company, or performance metrics, or educational attainment.

But many pay disparities are triggered by other decisions, which may or may not fall within these defenses. Some pay disparities are the result of market factors. For example, an employer may be constrained to offer a higher rate of pay to attract new employees, resulting in a situation where new hires earn more than long-term incumbents. Employers who take such an approach may find themselves facing legal challenges if incumbents contend such an approach results in a disparity. Discrimination claims can be brought when a seemingly neutral policy disproportionately affects a protected group (for example, women, minorities, older workers).

MOVEMENT TOWARD PAY TRANSPARENCY

The increasing awareness of pay inequity has also driven a movement toward greater pay transparency. Pay transparency can be described as the right to ask about, disclose, and discuss compensation. The corporate world is under pressure to improve pay transparency. Employees are demanding more information about their company's compensation arrangements, how their pay is determined, and how their compensation stacks up against that of others who perform the same or similar work. When companies provide more information about their compensation practices, employees can feel more confident that they are being compensated equitably. When pay practices are shrouded in mystery, employees wonder, "Am I being paid fairly?" Greater transparency regarding compensation is widely viewed as an important step in erasing remaining pay disparities.

State and local governing bodies are taking the lead in erasing the stigma of discussions about pay by enacting regulations that make it easier for information about pay practices to be available to employees and job applicants. What has emerged in recent years is a patchwork of pay transparency laws that vary by state.

The rapidly expanding list of state and local pay transparency regulations includes the following:

- prohibiting employers from asking applicants about their current salary or salary history
- requiring employers to include salary ranges of positions with their job postings
- requiring employers to disclose pay ranges upon an applicant's request
- expanding the prohibition against wage differences in "comparable work" (as opposed to the EPA term "equal work")
- prohibiting employers from limiting employees' right to discuss wages with one another
- prohibiting discrimination in wages based on protected classes other than gender

These provisions engender transparency. For example, if employers are required to publicly post the wage range for every available position, employees will be more likely to discuss their wages and compare their wages with that of other employers and coworkers. Posting ranges should limit the possibility that an employer will offer lower salaries to applicants who are not aggressive in pursuing the highest salary they can. These laws are viewed as likely to reduce pay disparity because all applicants will be on equal footing when negotiating their salary. It is well documented that women and minorities are less likely (than white males) to negotiate their starting salary according to research published in the *Harvard Business Review*.[3] When starting salaries start off skewed, disparities will increase over time when wage increases are based on a percentage. Researchers estimate that a pay gap of $1,000 at the start of a career can result in a cumulative loss of $500,000 over a career.[4] Regulations that require salary ranges to be posted should help address this disparity in starting salaries. Armed with a salary range, all applicants are on more equal footing in salary negotiations.

Laws prohibiting employers from asking applicants about their current wage or salary history are also viewed as a tool to help close gaps. The theory behind prohibiting applicant inquiries about their current salary is that employers often peg salary offers to applicants' current wages. If an applicant is paid under market, such an inquiry can perpetuate the underpayment. But if employers do not know what an applicant earns, they will be more likely to make a salary offer based on objective market considerations.

REMOTE WORKER SALARY

Should employers set salary depending on whether an employee is working remotely or works from an office?

The ability to work from home is viewed by some workers as a benefit, and some workers may be willing to earn less in return for the luxury of working from home. For those employers contemplating this two-tiered approach, think about what this practice messages to employees: Our organization places a higher value on employees who report to an office. Before promulgating a compensation scheme that discounts pay to remote employees, beware of the messaging. If your organization has made the decision to offer remote opportunities to broaden its pool of available talent, why pay remote employees less just because they work remotely? Such an approach may be at odds with your effort to attract qualified candidates.

The possibility of a disparate impact should also be considered. While the policy of paying remote workers less than their colleagues who do the same work in a nearby office appears to be neutral, what happens if most remote workers are women (who still assume a greater burden for household obligations including childcare and elder care)? If women are more likely to raise their hand and say, "I'll take the remote job and the pay cut," is the employer now vulnerable to a pay discrimination claim because the neutral policy now has a disparate impact on women?

Another question can arise regarding setting salaries for remote workers. If the organization considers geolocation, should the salary be determined by where the remote employee chooses to live or by the remote employee's assigned home office?

Basing salary on the local market is lawful. The cost of living in major metropolitan areas is typically far higher than the cost of living in a rural or exurban area. It is thus fair and reasonable for an organization to set salary based on geolocation. Companies that are agnostic as to where a remote worker works may want to abandon geolocation differences in pay. Likewise applying geolocational salary ranges based on a home office may not make sense when remote workers can work from anywhere.

In implementing a flexible work policy, leaders should consider how the policy will impact their organization's compensation scheme. Organizations that plan to put a premium on office-first work and pay commuters more should think through the various issues that will arise from this approach. Is the company prepared to lower the salaries of employees who move to remote status or increase the pay of employees who report to an office? If employees who opt for remote status and change their residence to a lower-cost location, will this result in a change in compensation? Or will the company freeze the salaries of existing staff who opt for remote work so that they gradually come in line with other peers in the same locations? What about a remote worker who moves to a location with a higher cost of living and the move was not at the employer's request? How these issues are addressed should be carefully considered to avoid creating even the appearance of pay inequity.

Action steps to create a fair compensation system include the following:

- Determine your organization's compensation philosophy.
- Set salary ranges for positions and adhere to the ranges.
- Conduct regular salary surveys to benchmark salaries.
- If geography will be a factor in setting pay, benchmark salaries on a geolocational basis regularly.
- Consider conducting a pay equity audit, but before doing so, consult with legal counsel.
- Ensure that practices are compliant with state and local regulations relating to pay transparency and pay equity.
- Analyze data relating to resignations; for example, are employees leaving for higher-paying positions?
- Consider information and data from your company's recruiters. Is your company's approach to compensation advancing its hiring goals?

DISCRIMINATION AND BIAS CLAIMS

In September 2021 the Equal Employment Opportunity Commission (EEOC) filed a lawsuit against an employer in connection with the employer's response to an employee's workplace accommodation request.[15] The key allegations asserted in the complaint were as follows. In March 2020, in response to the pandemic, the employer transitioned the aggrieved employee and others in her position to work remotely four days a week and report to their workplace only one day a week. In June 2020 the employer directed employees to return to the workplace four days a week and work remotely one day a week. According to the EEOC's legal complaint, the employee then sought an accommodation to work remotely two days a week. The justification for her request was that she suffered from obstructive lung disease, which made her more susceptible to COVID-19. The employer denied the accommodation request and shortly after that terminated her employment due to poor performance. The EEOC alleged the employer failed to accommodate the employee's disability and that other employees who held the same position as the aggrieved employee were permitted to work remotely more often than the one day per week provided by the employer's hybrid work policy. (We've streamlined and shortened the allegations here to simplify the discussion. As of this writing, the matter is unresolved.)

The case is a valuable discussion piece not only because it was the first post-pandemic case filed by the EEOC involving the administration of a hybrid work policy, but also because it presents a set of facts that leaders should pay attention to and learn from as they craft and administer hybrid work policies.

WORKPLACE ACCOMMODATION REQUESTS

Any discussion regarding workplace accommodations must include an overview of an employer's legal obligations and an employee's legal rights. We start with federal laws, which cover employers in all states.

The two key federal laws that establish workplace accommodation obligations are the Americans with Disabilities Act (ADA) and Title VII of the Civil Rights Act (Title VII). These laws apply to all employers of a minimum size (fifteen employees for Title VII and twenty employees for the ADA depending on the nature of the organization's business, though federal laws may apply). The ADA protects employees with disabilities by providing them with the right to an accommodation if one is needed to perform the essential functions of their job. Title VII permits employees to request reasonable accommodations to enable them to uphold their religious beliefs. So long as providing the accommodation does not result in an "undue hardship" to the employer, the employer may be required to provide an accommodation to enable the employee to perform his or her job. Without belaboring the legal issues, the accommodation need not be precisely what the employee requested; the employer may offer another accommodation that also meets the employee's needs.

State and local laws can broaden the coverage to employers of as few as one employee, so getting advice from an attorney or human capital expert is an important first step in understanding the legal environment in which your enterprise operates. In some jurisdictions (for example, California and New York), state and local laws provide a much more robust regulatory scheme than the federal laws and should be a key focus of compliance efforts.

An employee's ability to work remotely some or all the time has been a recognized accommodation for decades. For example, an employee who has mobility challenges may ask to work from home some or all the time to avoid the difficulty of commuting to work each day. Likewise, working from home on the eve of a Sabbath day might enable a Sabbath observer to work a full day if the employee cannot travel after sundown.

Before the 2020 shutdowns, many enterprises rejected requests from white-collar employees to work remotely or work from home on a flexible basis, taking the position that an employee's presence in the office was necessary. Many enterprises worked from this proposition and rejected requests to work from home from individual employees even when those requests were presented as a request for an accommodation when the employee had a disability or had to fulfill the obligations of their religious practices. Pre-lockdown, some employers could point to their complete prohibition against remote work as a basis to reject the accommodation. Now the calculation is completely different. Employers forced to migrate work from offices to employee homes in 2020 cannot dispute that their business can survive (and sometimes thrive) when employees are not together in an office.

THE EEOC'S LAWSUIT

The employee's allegations in the EEOC lawsuit demonstrate the potential legal pitfalls that enterprises now face as they institute and administer hybrid work policies. The request to accommodate an employee who has a disability (assuming this employee's lung condition is a disability) must be evaluated from the perspective of whether the requested accommodation creates an undue hardship to the employer. We could discuss the meaning of the legal term "undo hardship" for pages, but let's assume for the purposes of this discussion an undue hardship exists when it would be very expensive or significantly detrimental to the employer's business to allow this individual to work from home two days a week instead of one day a week. The factual burden the employer faces is convincing the jury that working from home two days a week presents an undue hardship when the employer voluntarily permits the employee to work from home one day each week.

As this employer has already committed to a hybrid schedule, how will the difference between working remotely one day a week as opposed to two days a week significantly impact this employee's ability to perform her duties? What facts can this employer produce to show that work from home one day a week does not hinder operations but two days a week is a problem? The employer has already invested in whatever technology is necessary for the aggrieved employee to work from home one day a week. The employer has already determined that work can be performed from home some of the time. It may be challenging for the employer to prove that accommodating the aggrieved employee's medical condition by permitting two days of remote work per week is an undue hardship if the employee worked remotely four days a week for several months and when the employer has already committed to a hybrid work schedule.

The EEOC complaint also alleges other employees performing the same job as the aggrieved employee were permitted to work from home more than one day a week. If true, this fact would create a legal hurdle for the employer. If other employees holding the same position as the aggrieved employee were permitted to work remotely more than the once weekly and permitted by the employer's policy, this fact would demonstrate that the requested accommodation does not create an undue hardship. If another employee could work from home two days a week, then why couldn't the aggrieved employee?

Here's the bottom line: The employer who denies a request to accommodate based on a protected classification has the legal burden to prove that making an accommodation would create an undue hardship. Employers should proceed with caution!

The analysis of whether an accommodation request to work remotely poses an undue hardship on the employer was forever altered when an enterprise permitted remote work during the 2020 lockdowns. If the organization responded to the pandemic by instituting remote work, that organization may be hard pressed now to take the position that remote work is an impossibility and poses an undue hardship. As the EEOC lawsuit illustrates, hybrid work policies may raise unintended potential legal issues relating to discrimination and accommodation. Consultation with human capital experts and employment law attorneys is a must for leaders as they navigate this new terrain.

THE APPEARANCE OF FAVORITISM

Hybrid work policies should democratize the opportunities for remote work. The opportunity to work from home even some of the time is viewed as an employee benefit. Granting it to some but not all white-collar employees could not only raise legal issues but also be viewed by employees as a fairness issue and could impact employee morale. There is a growing recognition that flexible work arrangements should be available to a broad range of white-collar workers. This is referred to as democratizing flexible work arrangements.[6] Democratizing remote work means recognizing that all white-collar work, not just the work performed by the most highly paid employees, can be performed on a hybrid or flexible work schedule. While no organization would promulgate a policy that allows only men to work remotely or only white employees, attention should be paid to the impact of flexible work policies that may have an unintended impact on employees in protected classes.

Leaders should take a critical view of their practices regarding remote work. Does the policy create flexibility for highly paid employees to work anywhere while requiring lower-paid employees to work in the office all the time? Such policies run the risk of creating a caste system where the educated elites have flexible work arrangements and less-educated employees are required to commute to an office. If this is your organization's practice, it is time to think carefully about why less-sophisticated work cannot be performed away from the office. Positions held by call center workers, administrative coordinators, and other nonprofessional employees in support roles can be handled successfully while remote. If your organization has designated these positions office-only positions yet it embraces hybrid work for marketing, sales, legal teams, and data analytics teams, your leaders should reconsider this approach.

Creating a hybrid work policy that limits the ability to work from home for only some positions can create the unintended consequence of discriminating against groups of workers who may be disproportionately represented in these positions. Let's illustrate this point with an example. An organization allows its white-collar workforce to work remotely or on a hybrid work schedule except for call center workers. If the organization's call center workers are largely women of color and its remaining white-collar workforce is largely male and white, does the remote work policy discriminate against women of color? Without additional facts, one cannot be sure. But one thing is certain: The policy feels unfair. Why can't call center employees—who are typically individual contributors who do not work collaboratively, and whose productivity can be readily measured by numbers of calls completed—work from home?

Consider another hypothetical situation. Assume an enterprise determines that its Marketing Department cannot work remotely. Marketing staff are required to work on a hybrid schedule and report to the office on a regular basis, perhaps two or three days a week. The justification here is that collaboration is the key to developing and implementing creative marketing plans. The Marketing Department is staffed predominately by women, most with children under the age of eighteen. This same enterprise has determined that the Programming Department is composed mostly of individual contributors who rarely need to meet in person because they do not engage in creative collaboration. As a result, programmers are not required to report to an office and can work remotely. Most of the programmers are men. Do these facts alone mean this policy discriminates against women or parents of school-age children? In March 2022 the EEOC issued guidance that focused on new issues relating to discrimination against caregivers in situations related to the pandemic.[7] In issuing the guidance, the EEOC noted that changes in work locations, schedules, and employment status required additional direction to employers navigating these new challenges.

The scenario discussed above does not provide adequate facts to determine whether the hybrid work policy might run afoul of an antidiscrimination law. But a member of the Marketing Department staff might wonder, "Why is it that I have to report to the office twice a week, but a programmer can live in another time zone?" Did the chief technology officer insist that the programming team have a fully remote option to ensure that a key employee who insisted on working remotely would not quit? Is the chief marketing officer a staunch believer in seeing her staff every week? The personal biases of these officers should be rejected as a basis for policy making. Instead, a neutral and bias-free approach should be taken. What if a Marketing Department employee requests to work remotely to accommodate her childcare obligations? How will the organization respond? Will denial of the marketing employee's request raise legal risks?

Leaders must be prepared to explain the basis for their decisions. And if the basis for the decision is something like, "This is what our policy says," is the explanation inadequate? And is that decision going to reflect the enterprise's culture, which is touted as supporting families?

Leaders should think carefully about making absolute decisions that may not withstand a legal challenge. Even if decisions stand up to legal challenge, they may be viewed as inconsistent with the spirit of flexible work and contrary to your organization's mission to be an employer of choice. Leaders should continuously ask if their policies promote equal opportunity and inclusiveness.

To be clear, there is no legal obligation to offer all positions the same hybrid work options. But your organization's decision to designate some but not all positions hybrid or remote-eligible must be able to withstand scrutiny.

In section I, where we discussed how leaders might approach developing a flexible work policy, we suggested that segmenting the work (and as a result the workforce) is a good starting point. As we noted, identifying what work could readily be performed away from the office is a critical early step in developing a hybrid approach. When segmenting the workforce, it is important to take a step back and question assumptions such as whether your organization believes that hourly employees should be excluded from any hybrid work policy.

If the reason leaders are reluctant to extend hybrid work opportunities to hourly workers is a lack of trust, this presents a significant opportunity to leadership. If leaders are uncertain whether certain parts of a business operation can be performed without the ongoing physical oversight of a supervisor, consider a pilot program to provide an accurate picture of the strengths and weaknesses of any decision. If we use the call center operation example, before moving all call center operations to a remote platform, first see how a team handles the work on a remote basis. Assess how well the team meets their targets when working remotely all the time, some of the time, or not at all. Then determine the feasibility of offering hybrid work arrangements (or remote) to employees engaged in call center operations.

The process of segmenting your enterprise's work is an important step in formulating a hybrid work policy. The segmenting exercise can help your organization establish policies that are based on operational needs and not biases.

HOW CLAIMS MIGHT ARISE
WHEN A POLICY IS NOT FOLLOWED

Inconsistent application of policies should be identified and corrected as quickly as possible. When leaders do not follow an established flexible work policy and instead dole out opportunities to work remotely or on a hybrid schedule based on favoritism, this inconsistent application of the policy can lead to internal complaints and worse yet, legal challenges.

What happens when leaders agree to side-deals with some of their employees? Not only will these arrangements (when exposed) raise fairness issues, they can also set the stage for discrimination claims. Consider this example. An organization's hybrid work policy requires regular presence in the office. An employee has arranged with their manager to work remotely despite the policy, and the manager has not advised anyone in the organization of this arrangement. Another employee on the team seeks an accommodation to work remotely due to a disability, and the human resources team denies the request, relying on the fact that all employees must adhere to a hybrid schedule. The employee seeking the accommodation then discloses the other employee's side-deal and accuses the organization of unlawfully failing to accommodate them. The employee seeking the accommodation points to the employee with the side-deal as support for a claim that the request will not create an undue hardship to the employer.

Leaders should be trained to understand the reasons underlying their policy and the importance of consistency.

PREVENTING DISCRIMINATION CLAIMS
RESULTING FROM HYBRID WORK PRACTICES

* Incorporate key elements of a flexible work policy. These will include reasonable guidelines; flexibility to enable leaders to make decisions based on unique circumstances; and accommodations based on disability and religious practices and any other classification where accommodations are required by law.
* Review the hybrid policy to assess whether the policy has unintended consequences that might be viewed as biased based on protected classifications.

- View hybrid policies as a way to democratize access to flexible work arrangements.
- Maintain a protocol for the consideration of accommodation requests.
- Include on your team legal counsel and human capital experts who are versed in the legal obligations relating to accommodations.
- Maintain records of accommodations requested and denied.
- Provide an opportunity for review of decisions to ensure legal compliance and internal consistency.

Chapter Nineteen

Avoiding Compliance Missteps

In mid-2020, as the pandemic shutdown changed from short- to long-term, organizations with white-collar workforces began to learn that many of their employees were working remotely from locations that did not match the home address they had on record. The migration of many employees to exotic and less-exotic locations far from city centers where the now-empty corporate offices were located had an unexpected impact on compliance issues. Enterprises were now employing workers who lived in many different states and not the state where their office was located. It took some time for organizations to realize that becoming a multistate (and in some cases a multicontinental) employer had unintended repercussions.

In the past decade, we saw an explosion in the number of states and localities issuing regulations governing the workplace. Local governments far outpaced the federal government in issuing new regulations affecting both large and small employers. This patchwork of regulations created unexpected issues for many organizations that were unaware that by expanding remote work opportunities for employees, they were taking on new compliance obligations. The result: a bit of a mess for employers who may have unwittingly walked into a maze of regulation by allowing employees to work from anywhere.

Hybrid arrangements create yet another potential compliance hurdle. State and local laws generally apply irrespective of how much work is performed in a locality. As a result, if an employee works from an office in Manhattan but works three days a week from home in neighboring

New Jersey, this employee may be covered by the laws of two different states as well as the employment laws that cover New York City–based employees. While there are exceptions, in most instances organizations should assume an employee working in multiple localities will be covered by the laws of all such localities. Keeping track of how many employees work from every location is important because many workplace laws are triggered by the number of employees working in the locality. This means that organizations must track not only how many employees work from an office but where every employee's virtual office is when they are not reporting to their office. It is essential that organizations maintain up-to-date information about where remote and hybrid employees are working. Without this information, organizations will not be able to confirm they are following the regulations of every applicable jurisdiction.

Almost every aspect of the employment relationship may be impacted by state and local legislation. Minimum wage laws may vary not just by state but in some instances by county and city and industry. Anti-discrimination regulations often expand the definition of a protected class far beyond those classes protected by federal law. Classes protected under federal law include race, gender, national origin, color, and religion (Title VII of the Civil Rights Act); age (Age Discrimination in Employment Act); disability (Americans with Disabilities Act and the Rehabilitation Act); citizenship (Immigration Reform and Control Act); and status as a veteran (Uniformed Services Employment and Reemployment Rights Act). But state and local laws may substantially increase the list of classes of employees protected by law. Such protected classes may include marital status; sexual orientation, expression, and identity; criminal history; status as a nursing mother; unemployment status; marijuana use; and hairstyle.

Further, state and local expansions of antidiscrimination laws may also broaden the definition of employer. Title VII of the Civil Rights Act of 1964 applies only to companies that employ fifteen or more employees. Local laws may prohibit discrimination by individuals not just companies and may apply to employers with fewer than fifteen employees. Counting the number of employees that may constitute the minimum for coverage by local regulations varies as well. Some laws require that all employees—regardless of location—be included in the count to determine whether a regulation applies, whereas other laws base the count of employees on where their employer is located.

Organizations granting requests from white-collar workers to work remotely must also ensure compliance with local laws regarding compensation. Minimum hourly wage laws vary widely across the country. A less-well-known fact is that minimum salaries also vary. While the Fair Labor Standards Act currently sets the minimum salary for exempt employees at $684 per week, the minimum is higher in some parts of the country, including New York, California, Colorado, Maine, and Washington. When hourly overtime-eligible employees work remotely, employers must ensure that they have protocols for employees to track the hours they work, and the employers should pay for all hours accurately tracked. In some jurisdictions, the local laws requiring meal and rest breaks include penalties for non-compliance that can be hefty. Making sure that accurate records are maintained is important wherever employees work, and the fact that employees are provided with some degree of flexibility does not excuse employers from these requirements.

Other pay legislation to watch out for are requirements that final pay (after a resignation or termination) be remitted within a specific period. Limitations on whether deductions can be made from pay and for what reasons and in what amounts also vary by location. There are even laws that limit how much can be recouped by an employer who erroneously overpays a worker (New York and Maine are two states that have legislated such limitations) or for wage deductions due to loan repayment obligations, personal charges on a company's credit card, or for overuse of unaccrued vacation benefits. (Keep in mind that this is merely a sample of the types of limitations on an employer's ability to make deductions from pay. The complete list of potential regulations is many times longer.)

The patchwork of leave law requirements is perhaps the thorniest. It is important that organizations with a remote or hybrid workforce identify the applicable leave laws and then take steps to ensure compliance. The types of leave laws that may exist in a jurisdiction might encompass leave for the following:

- blood donations
- court attendance
- COVID
- jury duty

- lactation
- illness
- parenting
- pregnancy
- domestic or sexual violence
- voting
- workers' compensation

Other workplace regulations that organizations should track include laws relating to training. Many states require sexual harassment training on a regular basis, and some states even direct the content of the training. There are state laws protecting employee privacy, including biometric information. Some states require employee access to personnel files even after the employment relationship has ended. Other state-specific requirements that may be important to an enterprise relate to the protection of trade secrets and the enforceability of restrict covenants—agreements not to compete or to solicit clients or employees once an employment relationship ends.

On a similar note, leaders must be sure that their enterprise's hiring practices comply with local requirements. Many states have enacted "ban the box" laws that prohibit applicant inquiries regarding criminal background. Likewise, we have seen an explosion of legislation prohibiting prospective employers from asking applicants about their earnings history. An even newer trend, adopted by the states of Colorado and New York City, requires employers to publish salary ranges with every job posting. There are penalties when these regulations are violated, so leaders beware. When extending the geographic breadth of your enterprise's recruitment efforts, be sure to consult with an expert with knowledge as to local laws.

Organizations should also take note of the potential tax consequences resulting from a remote or hybrid workforce. Some states require that the organization register to do business in the state once it becomes an employer of an individual residing in that state. Other states might not require a registration but will require the payment of state and local employment taxes, contributions to local unemployment benefit funds, and contributions to state-mandated workers compensation and other worker funds. Employers without a protocol to ensure they know where remote workers are working will inevitably run into issues with local taxing authorities.

A discussion regarding compliance relating to remote work would not be complete without consideration of international issues. Are any of your organization's remote employees working outside the United States? If so, it may be necessary, depending on the country and the length of time the employee will work abroad, to obtain a work visa. The enterprise could also experience tax consequences, again depending on the nature of the work performed by the remote employee and where the work is performed. Beyond the immigration and tax issues, there may be issues that can arise if the employee's activities in the foreign country result in permanent establishment risk—and the enterprise must pay taxes to the foreign government as a result of the presence of a remote worker. Generally speaking, permanent establishment risk can arise when an enterprise's business activities in a foreign country are deemed meaningful enough to translate into revenue to the enterprise. What a headache!

How to avoid compliance mishaps? Make sure your organization is aware of where its employees are working. We have noted the importance of intentionality. Here again, enterprises should not leave workplace law compliance to chance. Instead, they should put in place protocols ensuring that records regarding remote employees' residences are accurate. Some enterprises will make a decision that remote workers cannot work in certain jurisdictions because they deem the regulatory scheme of the certain jurisdictions to be too burdensome.

IDENTIFY AND UNDERSTAND STATE AND LOCAL EMPLOYMENT LAW REQUIREMENTS

Organizations that allow employees to work from anywhere must recognize the challenges attendant to engaging a national (or international) workforce. State laws regulating the relationship between employees and employers vary wildly. Avoiding unintentional consequences of employing remote workers requires a plan. Here are our suggestions:

- Identify a protocol for managing locations of remote and hybrid workers. Consider limiting remote and hybrid workers to certain locations.
- Promulgate a policy addressing remote workers' ability to work outside the United States.

- Identify individuals responsible for ensuring that your enterprise maintains compliance with state and local laws.
- Promulgate a protocol to ensure that recruiting activities are in compliance with the laws of the state in which the applicant resides.

Remember: The law of the state in which your employee resides will control legal obligations, and that could require your organization to comply with a plethora of state and local regulations that span every term and condition of employment such as:

- workers' compensation and withholding taxes
- sick leave entitlements
- minimum wage requirements
- minimum salary requirements for exempt employees
- frequency of pay requirements
- leave of absence requirements
- accommodation requirements
- final pay laws
- requirements to pay for expenses (phone, WiFi, etc.)
- right to review personnel file
- equal pay laws

Appendix
Training for the New Workplace

You can teach new tricks! Training is consistent with our theme of intentionality. The topics below reflect the suggestions we have made throughout these chapters to best arm leaders and individual contributors to succeed in a hybrid workplace.

Administer Your Hybrid Policy Fairly

- Knowing the Policy
- Understanding Accommodation Obligations
- Recognizing the Importance of Consistency

Diversity, Equity, and Inclusion (DEI)

- Defining DEI
- Emphasizing Your Organization's Commitment to Support DEI Efforts
- Understanding and Interrupting Bias
- Addressing Proximity Bias
- Understanding Micro-Aggression
- Finding Ways to Promote Equitable Treatment

The Importance of Enforcing Policy

- Protecting Confidential Information
- Making Sure That Hourly Employees Track Work Time Accurately

Meetings with a Distributed Workforce

- Getting Engagement from All Staff
- Preventing Zoom Fatigue and Virtual Platform Exhaustion
- Maximizing Virtual Presence

In-Person, Virtual, and Hybrid Meetings—Make Them Count

- Aligning Meeting Purpose with Structure, Participants, and Modality
- Knowing the Purpose of Pre-Meetings and How to Use Them
- Streamlining Meetings with Meeting Audits

Collaboration: The Essence of Teamwork

- Distinguishing between Asynchronous and Synchronous Work
- Aligning Collaboration Modality with Work
- Building Processes That Facilitate Cooperation and Productivity
- Coordinating Schedules and Styles

Performance Management as a Tool for Employee Development

- Clarifying Roles and Responsibilities
- Identifying Deliverables
- Developing Employees
- Using SMART Goals

Maximizing Productivity in a Flexible Hybrid Environment

- Exploring the Challenges of Meeting Deliverables with Employees Looking for Work-Life Balance
- Engaging Your Team to Shift to Goals Defined as Outcomes
- Identifying and Modifying Previous Assumptions about Work to Embrace a New Hybrid Model

Creating a Team Charter as a Tool to Align Culture, Processes, and Communication

- Defining Team Culture, Values, and Priorities
- Evaluating Current Processes and Communication Modalities
- Identifying Best Practices for Working Across Locations and Time
- Creating Guidelines for Use in Asynchronous and Synchronous Communication

Motivate, Engage, and Develop Employees with Feedback

- Understanding the Power of Praise, Appreciation, and Acknowledgment
- Using Creative Ways to Deliver Live and Virtual Feedback
- Knowing How to Give Negative Feedback
- Using Positive Feedback as a Growth Tool

Onboarding Steps from the First Interview to Team Integration

- Using Onboarding Practices to Ensure Engagement
- Defining the Role of the Manager and the Team
- Establishing Day-One Requirements
- Employing User Handbooks as a Tool to Help Acclimate New Team Members
- Monitoring the Onboarding Process Over the First Few Months

Creating Mentorship Programs

- Distinguishing between Formal and Informal Programs
- Understanding the Difference between Sponsorship and Mentorship
- Learning to Be an Effective Mentor or Mentee
- Defining Best Practices for Your Team

Managing Burnout

- Understanding Burnout
- Recognizing the Causes and Symptoms of Burnout
- Knowing Strategies to Help Avoid Burnout
- Putting Coping Strategies into Action

Embracing Hybrid Work

- Facilitating a Team-Change Management Program
- Supporting Individual Change Processes
- Creating New Procedures to Ensure Buy-In and Consistency

Mental Health and Wellness in a Hybrid World

- Recognizing the Challenges of Balancing Work and Life
- Being Flexible
- Respecting Boundaries and Rituals
- Remembering the Importance of Self-Care

The Art of Remote Supervision

- Knowing How to Develop and Stick with a Plan for Regular Check-Ins
- Communicating Expectations
- Supervising Not Surveilling
- Learning to Trust Staff

Coaching for Managers

- Developing Team Members with Coaching
- Problem Solving with Your Team
- Practicing Coaching and Performance Management

Guidelines for In-Person versus Virtual One-on-One Meetings

- Establishing Purposes and Objectives
- Recognizing Manager and Employee Needs
- Distinguishing between On-Going and Ad Hoc

Compassion in a Hybrid Environment

- Seeing Empathy, Sympathy, and Compassion as Leadership Essentials
- Using Compassion to Drive Engagement and Productivity in the Virtual World
- Putting the Power of Listening to Work

Glossary

Active listening: Listening that includes reflective responses and questioning while allowing the speaker to continue to talk.

Affirmative action employer: A company that maintains contracts and subcontracts with the US federal government and must recruit and advance qualified minorities, women, persons with disabilities, and covered veterans. Affirmative action includes training programs and outreach efforts. Employers that meet the definition of an affirmative action employer must have written affirmative action programs and must implement them, keep them on file, and update them annually.

Allyship: An intentional effort to address and erase any systemic racism, sexism, homophobia, or ableism that exists in the workplace.

Asynchronous communication: Any communication between two or more people that occurs at different times.

Automatic pilot: In a work environment, performing work as you are comfortable doing it and would have done in the past.

Big word: A phrase used by Julie Kantor to describe a word or phrase that has multiple meanings. Big words are overused and mean different things to different people within an organization and different things between organizations—for example, *own it, soon, collaborate, teamwork,* and *urgent.*

Boundaries: Separations between people, activities, demands, responsibilities, places, and times.

Bring your own device (BYOD): Arrangements in which employees are permitted to connect their own personal devices (phone, computer, tablet) to their employer's network and systems to complete job tasks either in the office or while working remotely.

Bring your whole self to work: Being comfortable enough to share your personal life, interests, and flaws with coworkers.

Burnout: A state of emotional, physical, and mental exhaustion caused by excessive and prolonged stress.

Check-ins: Meetings between a boss and his or her subordinates on a regular basis.

Cognitive bias: A systematic error in thinking that occurs when one processes and interprets information and affects the decisions and judgments they make.

Compressed workweek: An alternative work schedule that reduces a five-day, forty-hour workweek to fewer days. Typical options include four days of work, ten hours per day, and three days of work, twelve hours per day. A compressed workweek does not result in fewer hours of work per week; rather, it results in fewer days of work per week.

Confirmation bias: The tendency to look for and focus on information that supports and justifies the views one already holds. This leads individuals to interpret evidence in ways that support a pre-conceived viewpoint.

Deliverables: Measurable and observable services or goods that need to be provided by a certain date or time.

Digital inclusion: Ensuring that everyone, including financially and educationally disadvantaged groups, has access to and the skills needed to use the information and communication technologies that are necessary to participate in and benefit from an information society.

Distributed workforce: A business where employees work in different locations and circumstances; for example, employees of a single company may work at company headquarters, in satellite offices, in coworking spaces, or at home.

Drop-bys: Walking by a coworker or boss's desk or office to talk.

Exempt position: The duties and compensation arrangement for a position being such that employees holding the position need not be paid overtime compensation for more than forty hours of work in a regular workweek. This definition is set by the Fair Labor Standards Act and may be modified by applicable state and local laws.

Great Resignation, The: A social and economic trend in which employees voluntarily resigned from their jobs en masse beginning in early 2021. This was a socioeconomic trend that followed the widespread shutdowns mandated by the COVID-19 pandemic. Also known as The Big Quit or The Great Reshuffle.

Hoteling: A non-traditional method of office management used in lieu of permanent assigned seating. Typically, the workstation is dynamically scheduled.

Human capital: An intangible asset that encompasses the economic value of a worker's experience and skills. Human capital includes assets like education, training, intelligence, skills, and health as well as other characteristics employers value such as loyalty, punctuality, and corporate history.

Intentionality: Being deliberate, purposive, thoughtful, and mindful when making decisions.

Interpersonal glue: Personal connections ranging from superficial to intimate between two or more people that are based on nonwork commonalities, shared interests or activities, conversations, and vulnerability.

Intersectionality: Overlapping and interdependent systems of discrimination created by interconnected social categories. For example, the convergence of multiple social categorizations and identities such as race, class, and gender that results in magnified sources of bias and disadvantage.

Learning organization: A company that facilitates the learning of its members and continuously transforms itself.

Meeting inventory: Reviewing all meetings that an individual or team attends and evaluating them for priority, purpose, attendees, and time commitments. Using trends, add, subtract, streamline, or re-focus these meetings to maximize effectiveness and minimize wasted time. The goal is to streamline schedules and align an individual's or team's priorities with how they spend their time.

Microaggression: A comment or action that may be unconscious and unintentional that expresses a prejudiced attitude toward a social category. While the word *micro* defines something very small, micro-aggressions should be viewed as a meaningful and harmful demonstration of bias.

Micromanagement: In business management, a management style whereby a boss or manager closely observes, controls, supervises, or does the work of another.

Microtransition: Moving or changing from one activity to another during the workday.

Myth of Separate Worlds, The: The false belief that work and personal dynamics, commitments, and responsibilities are separate for each person.

Non-exempt position: The duties and compensation arrangement for a position being such that a daily record of work hours must be maintained to ensure that overtime compensation is paid for all hours worked over forty hours in a workweek.

Nonverbal communication: Communication via voice qualities, body language, and facial expression.

Office hours: A recurring period of time during each individual's workday or -week that allows coworkers and work associates to drop by, call, or communicate in any way without an appointment.

Pay equity: The movement toward erasing gaps in compensation that may be due to gender or race discrimination.

Pay transparency: The right to ask about, disclose, or discuss compensation.

PowerPoint-ese: A style of writing that uses short sentences, short paragraphs, and bulleted or numbered lists.

Pre-meeting: The time at the beginning of a meeting that is spent creating interpersonal glue via nonwork, off-task conversation.

Protected class: A group of people who share an attribute intended by a legislature to benefit from the protection of a statute—for example, Title VII of the Civil Rights Act covers the protected classes of sex, race, color, religion, and national origin.

Proximity bias: The mistaken assumption that employees who are physically present are more engaged and more productive. Proximity bias is a type of **cognitive bias**.

Psychological safety: Being able to be oneself without fear of negative consequences to self-image, status, or career. In a work environment, this means feeling safe to take risks, make mistakes, and speak freely.

Return to work (RTW): A socioeconomic movement that followed the mandated shutdowns associated with the COVID-19 pandemic and refers to the reluctance of white-collar workers to return to their office on a daily basis.

Rituals: Activities, conversations, breaks, celebrations, gestures, events, connections, and so on that occur on a regular basis and involve one or more people.

Round-robin lunch system: A grid schedule of lunch meetings that pairs two to three work associates for lunch. The goal is for coworkers to get to know one another better.

Self-care: The practice of workers looking after themselves that includes maintaining one's physical and mental well-being especially during periods of stress.

SMART: A well-established tool for setting and planning goals. The acronym stands for *specific, measurable, achievable, realistic,* and *time-based.*

Synchronous communication: Any communication between two or more people that occurs at the same time.

Team charter: A written agreement that is created by a team or department that includes guidelines for team functioning. Areas covered in team charters include communication standards, processes, meeting guidelines, clarity of roles and responsibilities, and hybrid work arrangements.

Train the trainer: A training framework and protocol whereby a group of prospective instructors are taught how to lead training sessions.

Video meeting: A type of online meeting in which two or more people engage in a live audiovisual call. It is a multidimensional communication modality that includes verbal messaging, visual cues, vocal quality, body language, and personal appearance.

Workforce segmentation: The process of identifying distinct groups of employees and designing human resources practices for each segment. This is typically done on a job level, hierarchical, or job-cluster basis.

Zoom ceiling: A glass ceiling for remote workers. This barrier affects remote workers when decreased in-office time impacts the individual's access to new project work, information, relationships, and so forth. These limitations may result in the individual being passed over for promotion.

Zoom fatigue: Physical, interpersonal, and emotion exhaustion that results from excessive time in video meetings.

Notes

INTRODUCTION

1. Partnership for New York City, "Return to Office Results Released—November," https://pfnyc.org/news/return-to-office-results-released-november.
2. Jose Maria Barrero, Nicholas Bloom, and Steven J. Davis, "Why Working From Home Will Stick," working paper 28731, National Bureau of Economic Research, April 2021, https://www.nber.org/papers/w28731.

CHAPTER ONE

1. Urbint, "We're on a Mission to Build a World with Zero Safety Incidents," https://www.urbint.com/careers.
2. Guðmundur D. Haraldsson and Jack Kellam, "Going Public: Iceland's Journey to a Shorter Work Week," Autonomy, https://autonomy.work/wp-content/uploads/2021/06/ICELAND_4DW.pdf.
3. Nicholas Bloom, "Don't Let Employees Pick their WFH Days," *Harvard Business Review*, March 25, 2021.
4. Eric Rosenbaum, "Biggest Risks in Return to Offices: Harvard Remote Work Guru," *Harvard Business Review*, April 29, 2021.

CHAPTER TWO

1. Kellen Browning, "Big Tech Makes a Big Bet: Offices Are Still the Future," *New York Times*, February 22, 2022.

2. Holden Walter-Warner, "Jamie Dimon to Work-From-Homers: You Win," The Real Deal, https://therealdeal.com/2022/04/04/jamie-dimon-to-work-from-homers-you-win.

CHAPTER THREE

1. Future Forum, "The Great Executive-Employee Disconnect: Study of Global Knowledge Workers Shows the View of the Office Looks Different from the Top," October 2021, https://futureforum.com/wp-content/uploads/2021/10/Future-Forum-Pulse-Report-October-2021.pdf.

CHAPTER FOUR

1. Bill Roberts, "Celebrate Differences," Society for Human Resource Management, December 1, 2012, https://www.shrm.org/hr-today/news/hr-magazine/pages/1212-employee-segmentation.aspx.

CHAPTER SIX

1. Frances Frei and Anne Morriss, "Culture Takes Over When the CEO Leaves the Room," Conference Board, May 14, 2012, https://www.conferenceboard.org/blog/postdetail.cfm?post=629&blogid=1.

2. Gerard J. Tellis, Jaideep C. Prabhu, and Rajesh K. Chandy, "Radical Innovation across Nations: The Preeminence of Corporate Culture," *Journal of Marketing*, January 1, 2009, https://doi.org/10.1509/jmkg.73.1.003.

3. Christos A. Makridis, "Here's the Proof Culture Still Comes First in the Age of Remote Work," *Fortune*, January 27, 2022, https://fortune.com/2022/01/27/heres-the-proof-culture-still-comes-first-in-the-age-of-remote-work-wfh-pandemic-managers-covid-employee-retention-christos-makridis/?mkt_tok=NzAy-LUNJSS01MDcAAAGCZKa92S1MFTP2sAQHm3iH8NTTZlGlc59yUKvscO Vdvb6OJWbpgzkKv3wlBN30aJMqwSJmwSM7ahblz2zdqpsi4fw0YDox7ZtY-w7jRKh9o7_U.

4. Charles Duhigg, "What Google Learned from Its Quest to Build the Perfect Team," *New York Times Magazine*, February 25, 2016, https://www.nytimes.com/2016/02/28/magazine/what-google-learned-from-its-quest-to-build-the-perfect-team.html.

5. Paul J. Zak, "The Neuroscience of Trust," *Harvard Business Review*, January–February 2017, https://hbr.org/2017/01/the-neuronscience-of-trust.

6. Randall Beck and Jim Harter, "Managers Account for 70% of Variance in Employee Engagement," Gallup, April 21, 2015, https://news.gallup.com/businessjournal/182792/managers-account-variance-employee-engagement.aspx.

7. Arianna Huffington and Jen Fisher, "It's Time to Replace Work-Life Balance with 'Life-Work Integration,'" *Fortune*, January 24, 2022, https://fortune.com/2022/01/24/great-resignation-life-work-integration-thrive-global/.

8. Carol S. Dweck, *Mindset: The New Psychology of Success* (New York: Ballantine, 2007).

9. Rebecca Deczynski, "Tracking Employee Satisfaction Is More Important Than Ever: These Tools Make It Easy," Inc., https://www.inc.com/rebecca-deczynski/employee-satisfaction-pulse-surveys-great-resignation-how-to-retain-employees.html.

CHAPTER SEVEN

1. William Bridges, "Bridges Transition Model," https://wmbridges.com/about/what-is-transition/.

2. Microsoft, "The Next Great Disruption Is Hybrid Work—Are We Ready?" https://www.microsoft.com/en-us/worklab/work-trend-index/hybrid-work.

3. Teresa Galanti, Gloria Guidetti, Elisabetta Mazzei, Salvatore Zappalà, and Ferdinando Toscano, "Work from Home during the COVID-19 Outbreak: The Impact on Employees' Remote Work Productivity, Engagement, and Stress," *Journal of Occupational and Environmental Medicine* 63, no. 7 (July 2021): e426–e432, https://www.ncbi.nlm.nih.gov/pmc/articles/PMC8247534/.

4. Nicholas Bloom, James Liang, John Roberts, and Zhichun Jenny Ying, "Does Working from Home Work? Evidence from a Chinese Experiment," *Quarterly Journal of Economics* (2015): 165–218, https://drive.google.com/file/d/1DPhkrgydBA7Xt9ZHHQv8ZcpBSbzgfy-F/view.

5. Jared Newman, "Why Companies Shouldn't Track Everything Their Remote Workers Do Online," *Fast Company*, https://www.fastcompany.com/90509420/surveilling-employees-who-work-from-home-could-do-more-harm-than-good.

6. The original source is a 1954 speech to the Second Assembly of the World Council of Churches; however, Eisenhower was allegedly quoting the president of Northwest University, Dr. J. Roscoe Miller.

CHAPTER EIGHT

1. Kelly Greenwood and Natasha Krol, "8 Ways Managers Can Support Employees," *Mental Health* (Mind Share Partners Study) August 7, 2020.
2. Cigna, "Loneliness and Its Impact on the American Workplace," https://www.cigna.com/static/www-cigna-com/docs/about-us/newsroom/studies-and-reports/combatting-loneliness/loneliness-and-its-impact-on-the-american-workplace.pdf.
3. BetterUp, "The Value of Belonging at Work: Investing in Workplace Inclusion," https://grow.betterup.com/resources/the-value-of-belonging-at-work-the-business-case-for-investing-in-workplace-inclusion-event.

CHAPTER NINE

1. Michael W. Kraus, "Voice-Only Communication Enhances Empathic Accuracy," *American Psychologist* 72, no. 7 (2017): 644–54, https://doi.org/10.1037/amp0000147.
2. Manyu Jiang, "The Reason Zoom Calls Drain Your Energy," BBC, April 22, 2020, https://www.bbc.com/worklife/article/20200421-why-zoom-video-chats-are-so-exhausting.

CHAPTER TEN

1. Doodle, "The State of Meetings 2019," https://doodle.com/en/resources/research-and-reports-/the-state-of-meetings-2019/.

CHAPTER ELEVEN

1. Neel Burton, MD, "The Difference Between Empathy and Sympathy: One Often Leads to the Other, But Not Always," *Psychology Today*, May 22, 2015, https://www.psychologytoday.com/us/blog/hide-and-seek/201505/empathy-vs-sympathy.
2. Michael Miller, "Why Empathy Is Your New Competitive Advantage," Six Seconds, https://www.6seconds.org/2021/05/31/empathy-future-work/.

3. Businessolver, *2021 State of Workplace Empathy*, https://resources.businessolver.com/c/2021-empathy-exec-summ?x=OE03jO.

4. Michael J. Dowling, "Embracing a Hybrid Workplace for Non-Clinical Staff," Northwell Health, https://www.northwell.edu/news/insights/embracing-a-hybrid-workplace-for-non-clinical-staff.

5. Ben Wigert and Sangeeta Agrawal, "Employee Burnout, Part 1: The 5 Main Causes," Gallup, https://www.gallup.com/workplace/237059/employee-burnout-part-main-causes.aspx.

6. Charles Duhigg, "What Google Learned From Its Quest to Build the Perfect Team," *New York Times Magazine*, February 25, 2016, https://www.nytimes.com/2016/02/28/magazine/what-google-learned-from-its-quest-to-build-the-perfect-team.html.

CHAPTER TWELVE

1. Kalle Heikkinen, William Kerr, Mika Malin, and Panu Routila, "4 Imperatives for Managing in Hybrid World," *Harvard Business Review*, June 28, 2021; https://hbr.org/2021/06/4-imperatives-for-managing-in-a-hybrid-world?utm_medium=email&utm_source=newsletter_daily&utm_campaign=dailyalert_notactsubs&deliveryName=DM139002.

2. George T. Doran, "There's a S.M.A.R.T. Way to Write Management's Goals and Objectives," *Management Review*, Vol. 70, Issue 11, pp. 35–36.

3. Jim Schleckser, "Why Warren Buffet Believes Feedback Is a Gift and You Should Too," *Inc.*; https://www.inc.com/jim-schleckser/why-warren-buffet-believes-feedback-is-a-gift-you-should-too.html.

CHAPTER THIRTEEN

1. Raffaele Carpi, John Douglas, and Frédéric Gascon, "Performance Management: Why Keeping Score Is So Important, and So Hard," McKinsey & Company, https://www.mckinsey.com/business-functions/operations/our-insights/performance-management-why-keeping-score-is-so-important-and-so-hard?cid=other-eml-ofl-mip-mck&hlkid=2fed01f886bc4df08d71e95e27467e99&hctky=13036892&hdpid=eb69c96f-23ec-4b1d-a570-3fcfd284c622.

CHAPTER FOURTEEN

1. www.flexjobs.com/blog/post/best-questions-to-ask-during-a-hybrid-work-interview.

CHAPTER FIFTEEN

1. *New York Times*, "Why Self-Care Isn't Selfish," January 6, 2021, https://www.nytimes.com/2021/01/06/well/live/why-self-care-isnt-selfish.html ?referringSource=articleShare.

2. Tom Nolan, "The No. 1 Employee Benefit That No One's Talking About," Gallup, https://www.gallup.com/workplace/232955/no-employee -benefit-no-one-talking.aspx.

CHAPTER SIXTEEN

1. Renee Obringer, Benjamin Rachunok, Debra Maia-Silva, Maryan Arbabzadeh, Roshanak Nateghi, and Kaveh Madani, "The Overlooked Environmental Footprint of Increasing Internet Use," *Resources, Conservation & Recycling* 167 (2021): 105389. https://impact-festival.earth/wp-content /uploads/2021/06/Overlooked-Environmental-Footprint-of-Increasing-Inte rnet-Use_2021_compressed.pdf.

2. Amanda Schupak, "Is Remote Working Better for the Environment? Not Necessarily," *Guardian*, August 2, 2021, https://www.theguardian.com /environment/2021/aug/02/is-remote-working-better-for-the-environment-not -necessarily.

3. Eric Friedrichsen, "Sustainable Post-COVID Business Travel Requires Corporate Action," GreenBiz, September 10, 2021, https://www.greenbiz.com /article/sustainable-post-covid-business-travel-requires-corporate-action.

4. CBRE, "Global Outlook 2030: The Age of Responsive Real Estate," https://www.cbre.com/-/media/files/global-outlook-2030/go2030_digital _final.pdf.

5. Future Forum, "The Great Executive-Employee Disconnect: Study of Global Knowledge Workers Shows the View of the Office Looks Different from the Top," https://futureforum.com/wp-content/uploads/2021/10/Future -Forum-Pulse-Report-October-2021.pdf.

6. Khristopher, J. Brooks, "Why Many Black Employees Don't Want to Return to the Office," CBS, October 26, 2021, https://www.cbsnews.com/news /black-workers-return-to-office-future-forum-workplace/.

7. Monica Torres, "Office Culture Is So Unwelcoming to Black Employees, They Don't Want to Go Back," HuffPost, July 17, 2021, https://www.huffpost.com/entry/black-workers-prefer-remote-work-racist -office_l_60c8f805e4b0f7e7ccf59fa1.

CHAPTER SEVENTEEN

1. Theresa Agovino, "The New World of Work," *HR Magazine*, June 2, 2021, https://www.shrm.org/hr-today/news/hr-magazine/summer2021/pages /the-new-world-of-work.aspx.
2. Society for Human Resources Management, press release, July 26, 2021.
3. Kathryn Dill, "WeWork CEO Says Least Engaged Employees Enjoy Working from Home," *Wall Street Journal*, May 12, 2021.
4. Corinne Purtill, "Can Workers Climb the Career Ladder from Outside the Office?" *New York Times*, March 3, 2022.
5. Patrick Thomas, "How to Gameplan Your Office Days: An Overachiever's Guide to Hybrid Work," *Wall Street Journal*, August 30, 2021.
6. LeanIn.Org, "Women in the Workplace: 2020," https://leanin.org /women-in-the-workplace-report-2020.

CHAPTER EIGHTEEN

1. Amanda Barroso and Anna Brown, "Gender Pay Gap in U.S. Held Steady in 2020," Pew Research Center, May 25, 2021, https://www.pewresearch.org /fact-tank/2021/05/25/gender-pay-gap-facts/.
2. Society for Resource Management, "SHRM Research Shows Pay Equity Pays Off for Employers," https://www.shrm.org/about-shrm/press-room/press -releases/pages/-shrm-research-shows-pay-equity-pays-off-for-employers.aspx.
3. Hannah Riley Bowles, "Why Women Don't Negotiate Their Job Offers," *Harvard Business Review*, June 19, 2014, https://hbr.org/2014/06/why-women -dont-negotiate-their-job-offers.
4. Christine Ro, "How the Salary 'Ask Gap' Perpetuates Unequal Pay," BBC, June 18, 2021, https://www.bbc.com/worklife/article/20210615-how -the-salary-ask-gap-perpetuates-unequal-pay.
5. U.S. District Court for the Northern District of Georgia, Atlanta Division, Civil Action no. 1:21-CV-3708-SCJ-RDC.
6. Joan C. Williams, Rachel M. Korn, and Mikayla Boginsky, "Don't Lose the Democratizing Effect of Remote Work," *Harvard Business Review*, August 4, 2021, https://hbr.org/2021/08/dont-lose-the-democratizing-effect-of-remote -work.
7. U.S. Equal Employment Opportunity Commission, "The COVID-19 Pandemic and Caregiver Discrimination under Federal Employment Discrimination Laws," https://www.eeoc.gov/laws/guidance/covid-19-pandemic-and -caregiver-discrimination-under-federal-employment.

Bibliography

Agovino, Theresa. "The New World of Work." *HR Magazine*, June 2, 2021. https://www.shrm.org/hr-today/news/hr-magazine/summer2021/pages/the -new-world-of-work.aspx.

Barrero, Jose Maria, Nicholas Bloom, and Steven J. Davis. "Why Working from Home Will Stick." National Bureau of Economic Research, April 2021 (Working Paper 28731). https://www.nber.org/papers/w28731.

Barroso, Amanda, and Anna Brown. "Gender Pay Gap in U.S. Held Steady in 2020." Pew Research Center, May 25, 2021. https://www.pewresearch.org /fact-tank/2021/05/25/gender-pay-gap-facts/.

Bloom, Nicholas. "Don't Let Employees Pick Their WFH Days." *Harvard Business Review*, March 25, 2021.

Bloom, Nicholas, James Liang, John Roberts, and Zhichun Jenny Ying. "Does Working from Home Work? Evidence from a Chinese Experiment." *Quarterly Journal of Economics* (2015): 165–218, https://drive.google.com/file/d /1DPhkrgydBA7Xt9ZHHQv8ZcpBSbzgfy-F/view.

Bowles, Hannah Riley. "Why Women Don't Negotiate Their Job Offers." *Harvard Business Review*, June 19, 2014. https://hbr.org/2014/06/why -women-dont-negotiate-their-job-offers.

Bridges, William. "Bridges Transition Model." https://wmbridges.com/about /what-is-transition/.

Browning, Kellen. "Big Tech Makes a Big Bet: Offices Are Still the Future." *New York Times*, February 22, 2022.

Carpi, Raffaele, John Douglas, and Frédéric Gascon. "Performance Management: Why Keeping Score Is So Important, and So Hard." McKinsey & Company, October 4, 2017. https://www.mckinsey.com/business-functions /operations/our-insights/performance-management-why-keeping-score-is

-so-important-and-so-hard?cid=other-eml-ofl-mip-mck&hlkid=2fed01f886
bc4df08d71e95e27467e99&hctky=13036892&hdpid=eb69c96f-23ec-4b1d
-a570-3fcfd284c622.

Cigna. "Loneliness and Its Impact on the American Workplace." March
2020. https://www.cigna.com/static/www-cigna-com/docs/about-us/news-
room/studies-and-reports/combatting-loneliness/loneliness-and-its-impact
-on-the-american-workplace.pdf.

Deczynski, Rebecca. "Tracking Employee Satisfaction Is More Important
Than Ever: These Tools Make It Easy." *Inc.* https://www.inc.com/rebecca
-deczynski/employee-satisfaction-pulse-surveys-great-resignation-how-to
-retain-employees.html.

Dill, Kathryn. "WeWork CEO Says Least Engaged Employees Enjoy Working
from Home." *Wall Street Journal*, May 12, 2021.

Doran, George T. "There's a S.M.A.R.T. Way to Write Management's Goals
and Objectives." *Management Review* 70, no. 11:35–36.

Duhigg, Charles. "What Google Learned from Its Quest to Build the Perfect Team." *New York Times Magazine*, February 25, 2016. https://www
.nytimes.com/2016/02/28/magazine/what-google-learned-from-its-quest-to
-build-the-perfect-team.html.

Dweck, Carol S. *Mindset: The New Psychology of Success.* New York:
Ballantine, 2007.

Friedrichsen, Eric. "Sustainable Post-COVID Business Travel Requires
Corporate Action." GreenBiz, September 10, 2021. https://www.greenbiz.com
/article/sustainable-post-covid-business-travel-requires-corporate-action.

Future Forum. "The Great Executive-Employee Disconnect: Study of Global
Knowledge Workers Shows the View of the Office Looks Different from the
Top." October 2021. https://futureforum.com/wp-content/uploads/2021/10
/Future-Forum-Pulse-Report-October-2021.pdf.

Galanti, Teresa, Gloria Guidetti, Elisabetta Mazzei, Salvatore Zappalà, and
Ferdinando Toscano. "Work from Home during the COVID-19 Outbreak: The Impact on Employees' Remote Work Productivity, Engagement, and Stress." *Journal of Occupational and Environmental Medicine*
63, no. 7 (July 2021): e426–e432. doi:10.1097/JOM.0000000000002236.
https://www.ncbi.nlm.nih.gov/pmc/articles/PMC8247534/.

Gallup. "Managers Account for 70% of Variance in Employee Engagement,"
April 21, 2015. https://news.gallup.com/businessjournal/182792/managers
-account-variance-employee-engagement.aspx.

Greenwood, Kelly, and Natasha Krol. "8 Ways Managers Can Support Employees." *Mental Health* (Mind Share Partners Study), August 7, 2020.

Haraldsson, Guðmundur D., and Jack Kellam. "Going Public: Iceland's Journey to a Shorter Work Week." Autonomy, June 2021. https://autonomy
.work/wp-content/uploads/2021/06/ICELAND_4DW.pdf.

Heikkinen, Kalle, William Kerr, Mika Malin, and Panu Routila. "4 Imperatives for Managing in a Hybrid World." *Harvard Business Review*, June 28, 2021. https://hbr.org/2021/06/4-imperatives-for-managing-in-a -hybrid-world?utm_medium=email&utm_source=newsletter_daily&utm _campaign=dailyalert_notactsubs&deliveryName=DM139002.

Huffington, Arianna, and Jen Fisher. "It's Time to Replace Work-Life Balance with 'Life-Work Integration.'" *Fortune*, January 24, 2022. https://fortune .com/2022/01/24/great-resignation-life-work-integration-thrive-global/.

Jiang, Manyu. "The Reason Zoom Calls Drain Your Energy." BBC, April 22, 2020. https://www.bbc.com/worklife/article/20200421-why-zoom-video -chats-are-so-exhausting.

Kraus, Michael W. "Voice-Only Communication Enhances Empathic Accuracy." *American Psychologist* 72, no. 7 (2017): 644–54. https://doi .org/10.1037/amp0000147.

LeanIn.Org. "Women in the Workplace." https://leanin.org/women-in-the -workplace-report-2020.

Makridis, Christos A. "Here's the Proof Culture Still Comes First in the Age of Remote Work." *Fortune*, January 27, 2022. https://fortune.com/2022/01/27 /heres-the-proof-culture-still-comes-first-in-the-age-of-remote-work-wfh -pandemic-managers-covid-employee-retention-christos-makridis/?mkt _tok=NzAyLUNJSS01MDcAAAGCZKa92S1MFTP2sAQHm3iH8NTTZl-Glc59yUKvscOVdvb6OJWbpgzkKv3wlBN30aJMqwSJmwSM7ahblz2zdq psi4fw0YDox7ZtYw7jRKh9o7_U.

Microsoft. "The Next Great Disruption Is Hybrid Work—Are We Ready?" March 22, 2021. https://www.microsoft.com/en-us/worklab/work-trend -index/hybrid-work.

Newman, Jared. "Why Companies Shouldn't Track Everything Their Remote Workers Do Online." *Fast Company*, May 27, 2020. https://www.fastcompany.com/90509420/surveilling-employees-who-work-from-home-could -do-more-harm-than-good.

Obringer, Renee, Benjamin Rachunok, Debra Maia-Silva, Maryan Arbabzadeh, Roshanak Nateghi, and Kaveh Madani. "The Overlooked Environmental Footprint of Increasing Internet Use." *Resources, Conservation & Recycling* 167 (2021): 105389. https://impact-festival.earth/wp-content/up-loads/2021/06/Overlooked-Environmental-Footprint-of-Increasing-Internet -Use_2021_compressed.pdf.

Partnership for New York. "Return to Office Results Released—November." November 10, 2021. https://pfnyc.org/news/return-to-office-results -released-november.

Purtill, Corinne. "Can Workers Climb the Career Ladder from Outside the Office?" *New York Times*, March 3, 2022.

Ro, Christine. "How the Salary 'Ask Gap' Perpetuates Unequal Pay." BBC, June 18, 2021. https://www.bbc.com/worklife/article/20210615-how-the-salary-ask-gap-perpetuates-unequal-pay.

Roberts, Bill. "Celebrate Differences." Society for Human Resource Management, December 1, 2012. https://www.shrm.org/hr-today/news/hr-magazine/pages/1212-employee-segmentation.aspx.

Rosenbaum, Eric. "Biggest Risks in Return to Offices: Harvard Remote Work Guru." *Harvard Business Review*, April 29, 2021.

Schleckser, Jim. "Why Warren Buffet Believes Feedback Is a Gift and You Should Too." *Inc.* https://www.inc.com/jim-schleckser/why-warren-buffet-believes-feedback-is-a-gift-you-should-too.html.

Schupak, Amanda. "Is Remote Working Better for the Environment? Not Necessarily." *Guardian*, August 2, 2021. https://www.theguardian.com/environment/2021/aug/02/is-remote-working-better-for-the-environment-not-necessarily.

Society for Human Resource Management. Press release, July 26, 2021.

Society for Human Resource Management. "SHRM Research Shows Pay Equity Pays Off for Employers." https://www.shrm.org/about-shrm/press-room/press-releases/pages/-shrm-research-shows-pay-equity-pays-off-for-employers.aspx.

Tellis, Gerard J., Jaideep C. Prabhu, and Rajesh K. Chandy. "Radical Innovation across Nations: The Preeminence of Corporate Culture." *Journal of Marketing*, January 1, 2009. https://doi.org/10.1509/jmkg.73.1.003.

Thomas, Patrick. "How to Gameplan Your Office Days: An Overachiever's Guide to Hybrid Work." *Wall Street Journal*, August 30, 2021.

US District Court for the Northern District of Georgia, Atlanta Division. Civil Action no. 1:21-CV-3708-SCJ-RDC.

Walter-Warner, Holden. "Jamie Dimon to Work-from-Homers: You Win." The Real Deal, April 4, 2022. https://therealdeal.com/2022/04/04/jamie-dimon-to-work-from-homers-you-win.

Williams, Joan C., Rachel M. Korn, and Mikayla Boginsky. "Don't Lose the Democratizing Effect of Remote Work." *Harvard Business Review*, August 4, 2021. https://hbr.org/2021/08/dont-lose-the-democratizing-effect-of-remote-work.

Zak, Paul J. "The Neuroscience of Trust." *Harvard Business Review*, January–February 2017. https://hbr.org/2017/01/the-neuronscience-of-trust.

Index

About the Authors

Julie P. Kantor, PhD: Julie P. Kantor, PhD is a business psychologist and founder of JP Kantor Consulting who has worked as an executive coach, advisor, and management consultant for over two decades. Her business experience, psychological training, and system analysis catalyzes individual and organizational change.

Julie works with a wide range of clients including small, limited partnerships; family businesses; professional service firms; and Fortune 500 companies. From big-picture strategy to daily functioning, she is the executive's ultimate resource.

She supports her clients in creating efficient, profitable, and trusting organizational cultures with programs that equip teams with practical tools they can immediately implement. Given the critical role of senior leaders in an organization, Julie works with top teams to simultaneously maximize individual member effectiveness and overall team dynamics. With her guidance, clients articulate clear communication programs, refine roles and responsibilities, and enhance processes. Her engagements include leaders transitioning to higher levels; executives building highly functioning teams; and individuals in need of improving problematic performance. Julie also partners with managers as they strive to help their direct reports turn around challenging individuals and situations.

She has authored more than fifty seminars that have trained thousands of employees on leadership, performance management, communication, and executive presence. Julie consulted with Columbia University on two class-action suits related to diversity and women's leadership.

Her research in the areas of resilience, emotional intelligence, and the intersection of work and personal lives date to her dissertation on dual-career couples. She has since used that expertise to help companies maximize their ability to celebrate differences, build inclusive leadership teams, and drive results.

Julie is a regular contributor to *Forbes* on leadership, coaching, and employee engagement. The *Wall Street Journal* has also sought her expertise. In support of strategic approaches to the future of work, Julie facilitates roundtables such as the Betsy Willis Architecture Foundation. She is committed to developing talent and serves as mentor through the Women in Cable Television organization.

Julie lives in New York City with her partner Jeff Molter. She cherishes her four children and their families who are scattered across the United States.

Felice B. Ekelman, JD: Felice B. Ekelman is a principal in the New York City office of Jackson Lewis P.C., where she practices workplace law on behalf of management. She is a former member of the firm's board of directors. Felice approaches the attorney–client relationship as a business partnership, and her clients rely on her to develop both legal and business strategies and when necessary to litigate bet-the-company cases.

Felice's employment law expertise is wide ranging. She is a counsellor. She provides regular advice to clients on a broad range of compliance issues including discrimination, workplace diversity, wage and hour and pay equity, disability and leave management, and issues relating to unionized workforces. She places paramount importance on understanding her clients' businesses, their goals, and their tolerance for risk. She conducts internal investigations and works with leaders in times of crisis and partners with public relations professionals. She has decades-long relationships with clients because of her ability to communicate with senior management, develop consensuses in problem solving, and work with clients to execute their goals. She is known for her ability to develop thoughtful and creative solutions to complex workplace issues, and clients trust her judgment.

When litigation is necessary, Felice stands at the ready. She has experience defending a broad range of employment law claims including the defense of discrimination and harassment actions. Felice has first-chair trial experience in a significant number of wage and hour class and collective actions as well as hundreds of matters in arbitration.

Felice is currently cochair of the board of directors of the Brooklyn Urban Garden School, an independent charter school with a curriculum that focuses on social and environmental sustainability. She serves on the board of advisers of the Johns Hopkins University Sheridan Libraries and Museums. She also is an adviser to Brighthire. Felice is the proud mom of two adult children who live near her and her husband in New York City.

CPSIA information can be obtained
at www.ICGtesting.com
Printed in the USA
BVHW040728121222
653961BV00002B/2